DEVELOPING *Connective* LEADERSHIP

SUCCESSES WITH
Thinking Maps®

GOVERNORS STATE UNIVERSITY
UNIVERSITY PARK, IL

Larry Alper • Kimberly Williams • David Hyerle

Solution Tree | Press

a division of

Solution Tree

555 North Morton Street
Bloomington, IN 47404
800.733.6786 (toll free) / 812.336.7700
FAX: 812.336.7790

email: info@solution-tree.com
solution-tree.com

Printed in the United States of America

15 14 13 12 11   1 2 3 4 5

Library of Congress Cataloging-in-Publication Data

Alper, Larry.

  Developing connective leadership : successes with thinking maps / Larry Alper, Kimberly Williams, David Hyerle.

      p. cm.

  Includes bibliographical references and index.

  ISBN 978-1-935249-72-6 (perfect bound) -- ISBN 978-1-935249-73-3 (library edition)

  1. Educational leadership--United States. 2. School management and organization--United States. 3. Visual learning--United States. 4. Learning, Psychology of. 5. Thought and thinking. I. Williams, Kimberly M., 1968- II. Hyerle, David. III. Title.

  LB2806.A526 2012

  371.2--dc23

                        2011030234

Solution Tree
Jeffrey C. Jones, CEO & President

Solution Tree Press
President: Douglas M. Rife
Publisher: Robert D. Clouse
Vice President of Production: Gretchen Knapp
Managing Production Editor: Caroline Wise
Copy Editor: Sarah Payne-Mills
Proofreader: Rachel Rosolina
Text and Cover Designer: Jenn Taylor

Thinking Maps® is a registered trademark of Thinking Maps, Inc. The trademark has been used with permission.

ACKNOWLEDGMENTS

We were compelled to write this book because of the stories of the leaders we profiled and of their colleagues; these leaders continue to inform and grow our work with Thinking Maps®. We would like to acknowledge all of them for their fearless and uncompromising efforts to improve leading, learning, and teaching for all members of their school communities. We want to especially thank Donna DeSiato, Judy Morgan, Jeff Matteson, Lynn Williams, Marcie Roberts, Ken McGuire, Cindy Slotkin, Kathy Ernst, Kevin Steele, and the research team at the Blackham School involved in this study for their generosity and insights.

We have benefited greatly from the work of Lloyd Jaeger in his many leadership capacities as he has both supported and guided the work with Thinking Maps in the area of leadership. The impact of his work continues to find expression in our thinking and in the work of others. We are grateful, too, for the seminal work of Art Costa and Bob Garmston in the development of the Cognitive Coaching model, which honors and supports the ability of people to become agents of change within their own lives and for others.

As you will see in the text, we have referenced the works of many authors. We have sought and found deep connections and insights from their writings for which we are grateful. We are especially appreciative of the work of Maxine Greene and Linda Lambert whose ideas never cease to inspire and challenge us. Their writing, drawn from a rich landscape that extends beyond the field of education, always invites us to "see things as if they could be otherwise."

We appreciate the support we have received from the team at Solution Tree who have encouraged, prodded, and expertly guided us through the process of writing this book. We want to thank Douglas Rife, Gretchen Knapp, and Caroline Wise who believed this was a project worth sharing with others in the field. We are especially appreciative of Sarah Payne-Mills for her patient and expert support through the final editing stages.

We would also like to thank our families for their endless support of our work. Larry would like to thank his wife, Kathy Ernst, who patiently read draft upon draft and provided honest and thoughtful comments. Her voice echoes in his.

Finally, we would like to acknowledge our own collaborative efforts and the commitment we made to tell these stories and search for the meaning within them. Together we share a determination not simply to report what has happened through this work but to try to understand why it has made a difference. In doing so, we hope that others will see in this work with Thinking Maps an opportunity to improve and enhance the educational experience within their schools.

Solution Tree Press would like to thank the following reviewers:

Pat Donaldson
Principal
Tusculum View Elementary School
Greeneville, Tennessee

Mary Ellen Hannon
Superintendent of Schools
Derry Cooperative School District
Derry, New Hampshire

Thomas Koch
Principal
Birchview Elementary School
Plymouth, Minnesota

Tim Lucas
Vice President, Leadership and Organizational Development
Performance Learning Systems
Allentown, Pennsylvania

Kaye VanSickle
Principal
Highland Elementary School
Baton Rouge, Louisiana

TABLE OF CONTENTS

ABOUT THE AUTHORS vii

PREFACE ix

Chapter 1: **A Brief Overview of Thinking Maps** 1

    A Language of Dynamic Cognitive Patterns 4

        Eight Maps for Eight Cognitive Processes 4

        A New Way of Asking and Answering Questions 8

        Five Common Themes 9

        Thinking Maps in Action 10

    A Language for Leadership 16

        We Need a Map! 18

    A Language for Connective Knowing 22

Chapter 2: **Thematic Strands in the Literature on Effective Leadership:**

           The Roots of Connectivity 25

    Emergent Leadership Themes 26

    Research on Effective School Leaders 28

        Create a Balanced Leadership Framework 29

        Clearly Define and Understand the Leadership Role 31

        Integrate Four Leadership Frames 31

        Build Leadership Capacity 32

        Embrace and Engage Diversity 33

        Excel in the Five Disciplines of Organizational Change 34

        Sustain Successful Leadership 35

        Broaden the Scope of Leadership and Contemplate Human Purpose 35

    Human Capacity 36

Chapter 3: **Leaders as Teachers: Facilitating Individual Learning, Growth,**

           and Development 39

    Walking the Talk 41

    Changing Power Dynamics and Empowering Others 45

    Seeing Clearly 48

        Acting Purposefully 49

Chapter 4: **Interpersonal Thinking** 53

   Enhancing Teacher Effectiveness 53

   Developing Skillful Thinking 54

   Coaching Professional Artistry 62

Chapter 5: **Collaborative Thinking** 69

   Working Toward a More Comprehensive and Shared Vision 70

   Leading Thinkers 72

      Becoming a Professional Learning Community 75

      Collectively Creating a Meaningful, Sustainable Plan 78

   Developing the Glue 81

Chapter 6: **Schoolwide Thinking** 85

   Networks of Learning Relationships 86

   Thinking Maps, Thinking Teams, Thinking Students, Thinking Schools 88

      A Language for Analysis and Reflection 90

   "Out of the Auditory": A New Kind of Meeting 98

      Thinking in Maps 100

      Developing Empowerment 102

   The Well of Emotions 105

   Universal Themes of Connective Leadership 107

Chapter 7: **Systems Thinking** 109

   Painting the Big Picture 109

   Teaching, Leading, and Learning in an Interconnected World 113

   Using Research-Informed Decision Making 115

   Becoming a Thinking School System in the 21st Century 116

      Leading Thinkers 117

      Shifting the Question 118

      Walking the Talk 119

   Connecting Multiple Voices, Multiple Minds for a Common Purpose 123

   Forming a Community of Learners and Leaders 127

   Achieving Clarity and Empowerment 133

   Achieving Sustainability 137

Epilogue: **Thinking by Design: The Act of Leading Thinkers** 139

REFERENCES AND RESOURCES 143

INDEX 149

ABOUT THE AUTHORS

Larry Alper is codirector of Designs for Thinking (www.mapthemind.com), an educational consulting group focused on research, cognitive development, literacy, and whole-school improvement through the use of Thinking Maps, a visual language for learning and leading. Larry is a former teacher and school administrator with more than thirty years of experience in leading schools and developing learning communities for students, teachers, and parents. For eighteen years, he was an elementary school principal in Brattleboro, Vermont. Early in his career, Larry and his wife, Kathy Ernst, cofounded an elementary school on Long Island based on democratic principles and student-centered learning.

As an affiliate of the University of Vermont's Asian Studies Outreach Program, Larry served as a director of the Institute on China and Its Cultures (Yunnan Province), an overseas program for teachers. He has traveled to China to lead groups of teachers throughout various regions and presented papers to Chinese educators on American educational practices at seminars in Beijing, Inner Mongolia, and the Yunnan Province. Larry has also been an adjunct faculty member at Antioch College. He is coauthor of *Student Successes With Thinking Maps.*

Larry received an undergraduate degree in elementary education from SUNY–Stony Brook and a master's degree in supervision and administration from the Bank Street College of Education.

Kimberly Williams, PhD, is an educational consultant who specializes in assessment, cognition, and improving teaching and learning. As a faculty member at the Plymouth State University College of Graduate Studies, Kimberly teaches graduate courses for teachers on cognition, history, and philosophy of education. She has also served on the faculty of the State University of New York at Morrisville and Cortland, Syracuse University, Hobart and William Smith College, and Dartmouth College. During her time with SUNY, she received awards for excellence in teaching and excellence in research.

She has written numerous articles on topics such as learning and cognition, drug abuse in adolescence, safety, violence prevention, and the social and emotional side of adolescent violence. She is the author of *Keeping Kids Safe, Healthy, and Smart* with Dr. Marcel Lebrun; *Socially Constructed School Violence: Lessons From the Field*; *The Peace Approach to Violence Prevention: A Guide for Administrators and Teachers*; and *Learning Limits: College Women, Drugs, and Relationships*.

Kimberly earned doctorate and master's degrees in education from Syracuse University and a bachelor's degree in psychology from St. Lawrence University.

David Hyerle, EdD, is an author, researcher, seminar leader, and keynote speaker focused on integrating content learning, thinking process instruction, and collaborative leadership across whole schools. He is founding director of the Thinking Foundation (www.thinkingfoundation.org), a nonprofit organization supporting research in cognitive and critical thinking development for the purpose of creating thinking schools nationally and internationally. The creation of his Thinking Maps model emerged from his experiences as a middle school teacher in inner city Oakland, California. His development of Thinking Maps was also informed by his work with the Bay Area Writing Project and the Cognitive Coaching model.

Among his numerous professional books and articles based on visual tools research, David wrote the foundational training materials for Thinking Maps and guided the professional development process with Thinking Maps, Inc. The Thinking Maps model is used in thirty states and six different countries. David cowrote the training guide *Thinking Maps: A Language for Leadership* and edited *Student Successes With Thinking Maps*, a professional book presenting background research and documenting the professional development outcomes from the implementation of Thinking Maps.

David earned a doctorate and bachelor's at the University of California–Berkeley and has served as a visiting scholar at the Harvard School of Education.

PREFACE

In the first phase of implementation of Thinking Maps across thousands of schools in the United States and several other countries from 1990 to 2000, the basic multiday professional development design focused on training teachers in whole-school faculties to use the maps to improve their own teaching while, most importantly, explicitly teaching their students across the school to use the maps as a common language for learning and assessment. We believe that if the students do not become fluent with Thinking Maps as their own language for learning, the implementation will remain at a superficial level. Extensive writing on the theory, research, and practice of Thinking Maps may be found in *Student Successes With Thinking Maps* (Hyerle & Alper, 2011) and *Visual Tools for Transforming Information Into Knowledge* (Hyerle, 2009). Practitioners' professional development training guides are used to foster the development of Thinking Maps across schools over multiple years. The primary training guide for teachers is *Thinking Maps: A Language for Learning* (Hyerle & Yeager, 2007).*

Thinking Maps have been applied deeply across all disciplines and grade levels from preK to college. Over time, they become a common visual language that unites a learning community around the focus on the explicit development of thinking skills and critical reflection. Professional development resources for improving writing, language development, and cross-discipline learning have been developed (as has Thinking Maps software) as schools have deepened their use of the maps. While this focus on the teacher-student relationship is still central, a new complementary strand of professional development emerged in the past decade as teachers and administrators began using the language for grade-level and faculty meetings, coaching, and a range of leadership practices. Over several years, many pilot sites began focusing on leadership using Thinking Maps, leading to the publication of *Thinking Maps: A Language for Leadership* (Alper & Hyerle, 2007). Most of the educators from the schools and school systems described in this book went through a minimum two-day Thinking Maps, Inc. training session in how to apply Thinking Maps to leadership practice. Most of these educators had already led the implementation of the maps in their classrooms and schools over many years.

The case-study analyses and examples we have included are based on a series of in-depth interviews and participant observations conducted throughout the 2008–2009 academic year with the leaders and schools profiled in this book. We gathered detailed field notes during the interviews and observations, which were analyzed for relevant themes and examples. Wanting additional time and space to develop their thinking, some participants shared written reflections. We have drawn from those throughout the book. In some instances, we have changed the names of participants and schools due to the confidential nature of the circumstances described.

---

*Note: Before utilizing Thinking Maps® as discussed herein, the educators highlighted in this professional book participated in required Thinking Maps training. Resources and training are provided by Thinking Maps, Inc. (www.thinkingmaps.com). Thinking Maps® is a registered trademark of Thinking Maps, Inc.

We also asked participants in the study to share artifacts—Thinking Maps—they had created as part of their individual and collaborative thinking processes. Many of these are included throughout the book to provide the reader with a visual record of the thinking that took place. Each of these maps started from a blank page or screen. They became populated with boxes and bubbles and circles and arrows as the people engaged in these processes literally drew out their thinking in a highly transparent and collaborative manner. They appear quite neat in the book, but don't let that deceive you. In the process of creation, they no doubt reflected the dynamic, messy nature that thinking truly is. Unlike a painter's finished canvas, the maps in process look much more like a painter's palette. The mixing of colors is perhaps an apt metaphor for the formulation of the emergent ideas in these processes. In the end, it all comes together, or you start over.

The leaders in this study were chosen not only because of their experience with applying Thinking Maps in their work as school leaders but also because they all were pushing at the edges of their practice. In choosing to work with Thinking Maps as they did, they purposefully entered into highly interactive relationships with those within their school community. In almost every instance, the people we chose to study recognized that their existing practices only approximated what they envisioned possible or desired in their work with others. They saw in the use of the maps, however, an opportunity, as Linda Lambert et al. (1995) propose, to "break set with old assumptions, and frame actions based on new behaviors and purposeful intentions" (p. 82). What they were reaching for—in a rather fearless manner—was greater alignment between the values and beliefs they held as school leaders and the practices they used to fulfill them. They chose to loosen the ground on which they walked in order to find a truer path. To do so, they needed a map, you might say.

Jeff Matteson, superintendent of the Canisteo-Greenwood Central School District, began the Thinking Maps process in his first meetings with his new leadership team. He made his thinking transparent and began the process of making it possible for others to do the same—from kindergarten to the school board level. Michael Sampson, superintendent of the Sedgwick Central School District, was asked to walk the talk and rescue an evaluation process headed for arbitration at the state level. His use of Thinking Maps not only saved a process from becoming protracted and potentially divisive, it did so in a dignified and respectful manner. It preserved the integrity of those involved with results far beyond their imagination. Superintendent Donna DeSiato and Executive Director of Curriculum, Instruction, and Accountability Judy Morgan of the East Syracuse Minoa Central School District decided that to truly prepare its students for the 21st century, the school district couldn't simply do better than what it already did. Donna and her colleagues believed they had to transform the very nature of the way people within the school district interacted with each other and the community in order to transform the learning experiences they offered to their students to meet these exciting challenges and opportunities. The stories from Ken McGuire at Bluebonnet Elementary School in Texas, Lynn Williams at

Yates Mill Elementary School in North Carolina, and Judy Kantor at Franklin Elementary School in New York—all school principals intent on building capacity within their schools for growth and sustainability—demonstrate that it is not enough to distribute leadership; it is necessary to cultivate the ability within groups and individuals to enact it skillfully and effectively. The account of the work of the Vertical Data Team at Blackham School in Bridgeport, Connecticut, describes the actions this group of teacher leaders has taken to use Thinking Maps as leadership tools and to improve their ability to fulfill their leadership responsibilities. This compelling story demonstrates how the use of the maps to develop their capacity as leaders helped the teachers directly and indirectly improve student learning in their school in the process.

In all of the case studies woven throughout this book, we will be hearing from school leaders and visiting schools where Thinking Maps have animated the idea of leading connectively. After giving an introduction to Thinking Maps in chapter 1, we will contextualize this language for leading and learning within a new array of leadership theories and practices in chapter 2. Then we turn to how these themes emerge from the layers of human connection we all feel within the process of leading and thinking: from personal reflectiveness (chapter 3), to interpersonal interactions and coaching (chapter 4), to group dynamics (chapter 5), to schoolwide change processes (chapter 6), and finally, to transformative processes at the school-system level (chapter 7). The epilogue will bring us back to the act of leading thinkers: engaging our capacity to connect the dots within ourselves and see more clearly the power of collaboratively drawing out meaningful, connective thinking in maps.

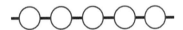

There have been over 20,000 books published about leadership. One has to appreciate the degree to which this topic of leadership has been researched, documented, and theorized. Such close attention and study perhaps pay tribute to the complexity and critical role of leadership in the growth of and change in organizations. A common finding or conclusion in all of these studies is that leadership makes a difference, and effective leadership has the potential to transform lives. Naturally, then, we want to know and understand how and why the practices of leadership have such a profound impact on people and organizations.

With great respect for this vast field of research, we dared to further populate it with a new study. However, we were inspired to do so by the compelling nature of the stories from people who had begun to use Thinking Maps in their leadership practice, even, in some cases, before their use in this area had been formally articulated. As we heard and gathered these stories, it became evident that common themes were emerging across different settings and diverse applications of this work. It became apparent, too, that while the emergent themes were not totally unfamiliar, new dimensions to these themes were being revealed through the use of Thinking Maps. For these reasons and more, we felt it was important to bring this work forward and invite others to consider the contributions this work might make to the field of educational change and school-improvement efforts.

A Brief Overview of Thinking Maps

What is compelling to me about the act of drawing is that you become aware, or conscious of, what you're looking at only through the mechanism of trying to draw it. When I look at something, I do not see it unless I make an internal decision to draw it. Drawing it in a state of humility provides a way for truth to emerge.

—MILTON GLASER

To connect is one of our most fundamental human impulses—not just with others on a personal level, but with ideas as well. We are, as many brain researchers have noted, pattern seekers and meaning makers. In fact, in large part, it has been through the recognition of patterns that we have survived and flourished. To be a human being is to be connected to others, to be engaged with others in pairs, groups, families, and communities toward common goals, and ultimately to engage in the balancing act of improving the well-being of ourselves and others. As Margaret Wheatley (1999) observes, "Everything comes into form because of relationships. We are constantly called to be in a relationship—to information, people, events, ideas, life" (p. 145). In another context she adds, "The instinct of community is everywhere in life" (2005, p. 47).

Schools are institutions built on an assumed outcome of continuous positive growth for the betterment of students and society, much like medical institutions that constantly attend to the physical and emotional well-being of people. Yet too often when individual leaders and leadership groups engage in the process of thinking through problems, making decisions, and evaluating outcomes, we find ourselves *disconnected*. During many one-on-one conversations, small-group discussions, faculty meetings, and professional development sessions, the conversations may begin well, but then fall prey to people taking positions, rolling out their emotional states and logical arguments, and wielding power based in raw authority rather than in mindful, thoughtful judgments. People in these situations often feel embattled and separated from others—as if the face of a colleague across the table or across the hall is that of an adversary, rather than an ally on the same journey.

A challenge that leaders face, then, is how to dynamically surface thinking and identify actions in a way that allows ideas to be reformulated or reconstructed in a pluralistic environment. How do we bring discovery into the context of our interactions in a way that energizes and inspires insight and innovation? How do we become consciously aware of knowing ourselves in patterns of relationships within challenging decision-making conflicts? After all, empathy starts within. Over many years of reflective practice in schools and through research in psychology and the cognitive neurosciences, we are now more aware of how we are unconsciously self-deceiving: our individual, ever-changing brain structures have been wired tight, frozen in some instances by our past experiences and the schemas that frame our thinking. Look into Daniel Goleman's (1985) first book, *Vital Lies, Simple Truths: The Psychology of Self-Deception*, for a full analysis of how our emotions and cognitive states of mind deeply influence our capacities to see ourselves and others with an open mind. "Schemas are the ghost in the machine," Goleman (1985, p. 75) writes, for these connected patterns drawn from experience, substantiated and reinforced in our minds, drive our perceptions of the moment and prevent transformational thinking and actions.

For example, when we sit in or lead a faculty meeting, we already have a frame of reference for what a faculty meeting is about: a mixture of good, bad, and indifferent drawn from a career of faculty meetings. Faculty meetings may also bring up past experiences of family meetings. We bring to our concept of *faculty meeting* our own mindsets, relationships, and established mental and emotionally connected imprinted patterns that are the perceptual windows through which we see what is happening and what we expect to happen. Our brains actively seek to see what we already know. We are comforted by replaying the same recording even if the repeating story is negative. The capacity for each of us as individuals and then collectively to identify the existing *frames* that ground our perceptions and actions—and to consciously reframe and repattern our ways of thinking—is a key to creating participatory, connective leadership in one-on-one conversations, grade-level meetings, and large-group sessions such as faculty meetings.

Connective leading is about fostering the connections between and among people, between and among ideas within patterns of thinking, and across visual and virtual planes, which the diversity of those present and represented inform and enrich. To lead connectively means to invite possibilities into the process with the bold and confident view that, by design, the collective wisdom of the community of learners will emerge, and from this, effective and meaningful solutions will be determined. Connective leading requires skillful facilitation because it is about interconnecting people in the complex dance of both personal and professional conversations. This critical dimension of leadership is expressed in all aspects of the school community—classroom, meeting room, and boardroom. As the case studies in our research will demonstrate in later chapters, the culture of the school transforms as school leaders model the very same approaches and dispositions that they expect all learners, adults and students, to use.

Connective leading requires a significant leap of faith, a fearlessness, and a confidence in self and others in the face of emerging truths—perhaps even uncomfortable realities. The decision to become open to possibilities and to initiate the dynamic interaction between self and others, mind and experience, can be as unsettling as it is exciting. The humility that Glaser proposes in the epigraph is key; the suspension of ego and attachment to particular points of view and interpretations forms the necessary ground from which the truth, so to speak, can emerge (Glaser, 2008).

But remaining open to our own perceptions—which means to consciously hold lightly our own point of view—while deeply listening to and reflecting on what our colleagues are saying and doing is *extremely* difficult. Just try listening closely to another person without your internal dialogue interrupting the other person's words even before you verbally interrupt the person speaking! We so deeply want to connect to what other people are saying in the moment, but often our own stories prevent or constrain a constructive openness to future possibilities. We have a tendency to listen for affirmation of our own ideas.

Presently, this concept of being connected surfaces in the field of the cognitive neurosciences and, interestingly, overlaps with the global media network of connections. Networks exist in the brain, in the mind, between people, and virtually around the globe. We now know that the brain is constantly and unconsciously making neural connections between the nodes: constructing, deconstructing, and reinforcing neural networks and making patterns from sensory information drawn in from outside the body. The human mind is also making *cognitive* connections and consciously (or unconsciously) seeking and creating cognitive patterns based on a synthesis of what the brain already has imprinted within its neural circuitry from a lifetime of experiences. Consider the idea of making connections as an umbrella synthesis of neural connections, patterns of mind, and digital web-based links. We are connected around the globe from a handheld device.

If we can learn anything from this new synthesis of the networking brain, mind, and world, it is that communication now depends on our capacity to seek, create, and make *connections*. Paradoxically, with greater understanding about how the brain works and the pathways for connecting and communicating, we may have a simultaneous sense of disconnection. This may be because we have no new pathways or languages for showing how we actively pattern ideas and represent connected thinking as meaningful knowledge. There are so many networks of connections, but so few ways to fully express the wholeness of our thinking. We have no language for connecting nonlinear bits of information that represent both our minds at work and the rich networking capacities of our brain and our web-based communication systems. We are, simply, framed by our existing representation systems of speaking and writing. True, we send each other more pictures and video downloads. However, almost all of our messages are oddly still linear strings of words—voice and text messages, tweets of 140 characters, quickly written blogs, email and text documents, and bulleted PowerPoint slides with visual eye candy—and while we sit in faculty meetings, we exchange spoken strings of words and pages upon pages of announcements. This is all good in many ways, but it also has brought about cognitive overload and distraction, overwhelming us with disconnected bits of information and disconnected knowledge.

As teachers focused on learning and leaders focused on leading learning, we have primarily depended on the spoken and written word to convey what and how we think. Across districts, schools, and classrooms, we state what we think in strings of words; we write memos, emails, and reports, and we create long, often inaccessible strategic plans. Words, while powerful, are only the tip of the iceberg for the rich connected patterns of thinking bound in the deeper structures of spoken language and written texts, concepts, and schemata. Our ideas are borne in dynamic, complex, multilayered, and differentiated patterns of thinking, but usually we are forced to articulate them in sound bites and data bits. So how do we, as educator leaders responsible for relaying high-quality communication every day to students, work to see and show other people our own connected patterns while seeking out and seeing others' points of view? If our best thinking comes by making connections and building patterns, then what would these patterns look like, and what might they be based on?

A Language of Dynamic Cognitive Patterns

Thinking Maps are not a program or a model or simply a loose collection of useful graphics. Thinking Maps are, by definition, a *language*. Languages are symbolic systems comprised of agreed-on graphic marks that, combined together, enable humans to communicate simple to ever-more-complex thoughts with elegance and efficiency. Human beings traffic in symbols: they are the way we think, learn, and communicate. Every symbolic system or language has a purpose: the exchange of information and knowledge, whether it is literary, musical, mathematical, scientific, or artistic. Think of the eight parts of speech that constitute our English language, the numbers 0 to 9 in mathematics, musical and scientific notations, Braille, and even computer code.

Thinking Maps are a graphic cognitive code that helps us visually represent patterns of thinking as interdependent mental models: to combine and synthesize the internal thinking patterns of participants in a classroom, leadership group, or boardroom. The common visual language of Thinking Maps can be used in any learning community to explicitly, visually represent the connections we make as individuals. This language may be used across any field, but within the field of education, students, teachers, and administrators draw these dynamic graphics on blank pages so that they may individually and collaboratively *draw out* their creative and analytical thinking, whether in the teaching, learning, and assessment cycle or for communicating and problem solving. Thinking Maps can be used in a coaching or supervisory context, in small groups such as grade-level teams, in large faculty gatherings, and across the whole school over time.

Eight Maps for Eight Cognitive Processes

The language of Thinking Maps is used to symbolically represent, define, and activate eight specific, interdependent cognitive processes as visual-verbal patterns. These eight processes have been repeatedly identified through seventy years of cognitive science research as being fundamental operations of the human mind and brain. Tests of intelligence, models of cognitive processes, and "thinking skills" programs that researchers have developed rely on these eight processes. (A comprehensive review of these models and programs may be found in *Developing Minds* [Costa, 2001]. Bloom's taxonomy of educational objectives identified macroprocesses, such as the analysis and synthesis required for developing high-quality learning structures. The underlying cognitive processes, such as describing, comparing, categorizing, and seeing causes and effects, are the fundamental, interdependent operations necessary for reaching the macro objectives Bloom and others have identified.) The eight processes are:

1. Defining in context (labeling, definition)

2. Describing qualities (properties, characteristics, attributes)

3. Comparing and contrasting (similarities, differences)

4. Classification (classification, categorization, grouping)

5. Part-whole (spatial reasoning, physical structures)

6. Sequencing (ordering, seriation, cycles)

7. Cause-effect (causality, prediction, systems feedbacks)

8. Analogies (analogy, simile, metaphor, allegory)

From the early days of intelligence testing, understanding these eight processes has been instrumental in identifying strengths and weaknesses in logical reasoning; they are also foundational in the areas of curriculum design and development, teaching, and standards-based testing.

Jean Piaget (Piaget & Inhelder, 1969) more clearly recognizes these processes as dynamic *mental operations* that are with us from our first days through early childhood and stay with us and grow in levels of abstraction and complexity throughout our lifetime. These are not simple logical operations, but mental operations that require creative, interpretive, and reflective thinking. Our capacity for complexity in each individual cognitive process grows through adulthood, but more importantly, through combination and interdependency of the eight processes, our capacity for complex thinking and reflectiveness also grows. Piaget believes that through the overlapping stages of development, all of these processes become ever more intertwined and enable complex thinking and higher levels of abstraction. These are not lower-order thinking skills that we abandon for higher-order skills: learners continue to use each of the eight processes at ever higher levels of complexity and combine them all to create, with content, the richness of ideas and concepts.

Unfortunately, this cognitive code is not often made explicit to learners, whether children or adults. While some thinking-skills programs, many curriculum materials, and even the core standards use these terms, learners rarely develop a conscious, independent, and high degree of mental fluency when using them. Furthermore, the processes are most often represented as strictly *verbal*. The Thinking Maps language brings together the basic definition of these processes as verbal-*visual* patterns.

There are eight different Thinking Maps forms that align with these eight cognitive skills (see figure 1.1). Each map has a simple form (the graphic primitives shown on the left in the figure) and an expanded form (shown on the right). The maps are iterative and fractal, much like the branch and leaf structure of trees in nature or any organic structure. Their expansion from primitive to complex forms reflects what Michael Fullan references as *simplexity*: the capacity we need as leaders and learners to think about, learn, communicate, and discuss complex systems simply and clearly, not simplistically (Fullan, 2010).

The processes of fully integrating Thinking Maps across a whole school often begins with professional development for all teachers and administrators in how to directly teach students to use each map in isolation and, importantly, together as interdependent tools. During the first full day of professional development, teachers and administrators learn the theory of Thinking Maps. They learn about and experience each of the eight Thinking Maps and the Frame of Reference, and they leave with a plan for systematically introducing the language to their students and integrating the maps across all content areas. Subsequent professional development deepens and extends their knowledge and fluency with Thinking Maps and associates the work across the curriculum, state and national standards, and other contexts within the school. The professional development is also designed to connect with those areas that the school has identified as areas of particular need or interest. Importantly, the first day of training, along with follow-up classroom support, focuses on understanding the direct link between a fundamental cognitive process and a corresponding graphic primitive by creating applications from either a blank page, whiteboard, or computer screen; practicing how to select one or multiple maps as related to questions teachers ask students related to content standards and processes, such as reading and writing; transferring all maps across disciplines and the teaching of content information and conceptual understandings; and improving their capacity to teach every student how to become fluent with Thinking Maps as a language for learning in a collaborative classroom setting.

This is analogous to a carpenter developing deep skill with each of the basic tools in his or her toolbox as well as knowing how to use all of the tools together in the longer processes of construction. In the case of Thinking Maps, students, teachers, and school leaders construct knowledge from eight fundamental *mental* tools for patterning information and framing the structures of creative, analytic, and conceptual knowledge. As people move from novice to expert use of the Thinking Maps, they are developing what Bloom (1986) calls *automaticity* with the maps as a language for their own use, and not merely as isolated graphics that they designate for specific assignments.

The first step that teachers take after the initial professional development training is to teach the maps to students. This is done through very simple activities of applying each map to an object, such as an apple, or through guiding students to use each map for an autobiography. Ideally, the next step would be to assess each student's fluency with each cognitive process and his or her abilities to apply the map in a specific content area.

Primitives	**Thinking Maps and the Frame of Reference**	**Expanded Maps**
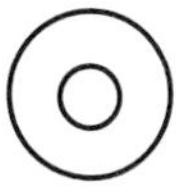	The Circle Map is used for seeking context. This tool enables learners to generate relevant information about a topic as represented in the center of the circle. This map is often used for brainstorming.	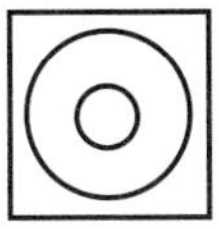
	The Bubble Map is designed for the process of describing attributes. This map is used to identify character traits (language arts), cultural traits (social studies), properties (sciences), or attributes (mathematics).	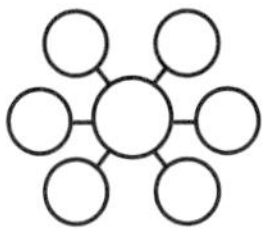
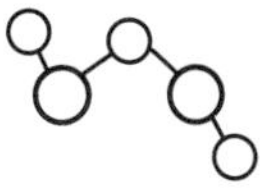	The Double Bubble Map is used for comparing and contrasting two things, such as two characters in a story, two historical figures, or two social systems. It is also used for prioritizing what information is most important in a comparison.	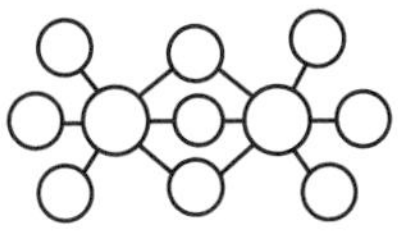
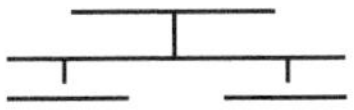	The Tree Map enables learners to do both inductive and deductive classification. People learn to create general concepts, (main) ideas, or category headings at the top of the tree and supporting ideas and specific details in the branches below.	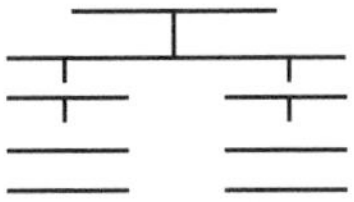
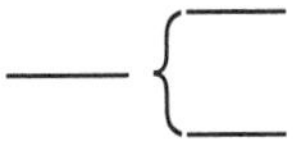	The Brace Map is used for identifying the part-whole, physical relationships of an object. By representing part-whole and part-subpart relationships, this map supports learners' spatial reasoning and their understanding of how to determine physical boundaries.	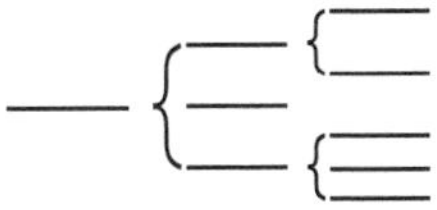
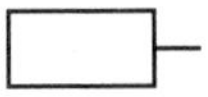	The Flow Map is based on the use of flowcharts. Learners use it to show sequences, order, timelines, cycles, actions, steps, and directions. This map also focuses students on seeing the relationships between stages and substages of events.	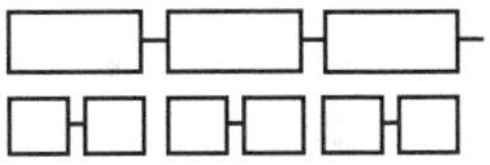
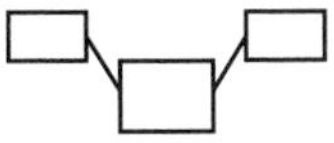	The Multi-Flow Map is a tool for seeking the causes and effects of events. The map expands when showing historical causes and predicting future events and outcomes. In its most complex form, it expands to show the interrelationships of feedback effects in a dynamic system.	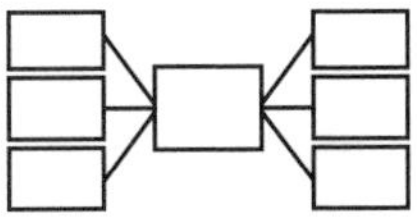
	The Bridge Map provides a visual pathway for creating and interpreting analogies. Beyond the use of this map for solving analogies on standardized tests, this map is used for developing analogical reasoning and metaphorical concepts for deeper content learning.	
	The Frame of Reference The metacognitive Frame is not one of the eight Thinking Maps. It may be drawn around any of the maps at any time as a *metatool* for identifying and sharing one's frame of reference for the information found within one of the Thinking Maps.	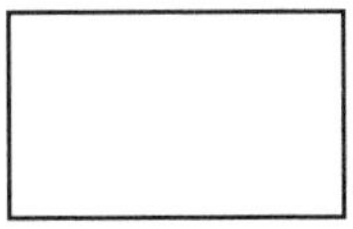

Source: Hyerle & Alper, 2006.

Figure 1.1: Defining the eight Thinking Maps and the Frame of Reference.

Once teachers introduce, model, and reinforce the maps over several years, students develop fluency with each map; they are able to transfer multiple maps into each content area and become spontaneous in their ability to choose and use the maps for whatever content information and concept they are learning. This also enables students to use Thinking Maps to see *their own* thinking patterns for self-assessment and share their maps or combine them with peers' in cooperative groups; the maps also offer an effective way for teachers to effectively assess individual content knowledge and concepts. Teachers may ask students to use the map before, during, and after a lesson or unit of study. While this process is going on, teachers, teacher assistants, support staff, and school leaders are also developing fluency with Thinking Maps for their own professional growth, communication, collaboration, and leadership practices at higher degrees of sophistication and complexity.

Since the early piloting and development of the professional development guide *Thinking Maps: A Language for Leadership* (Alper & Hyerle, 2007), school teams and faculties have a resource for systematic training in the explicit use of Thinking Maps as a common visual language for learning communities. Uniting students, teachers, and administrators across a whole school with a highly adaptable, transferrable language for thinking, communicating, problem solving, decision making, and assessing is unique in the field of education. When students see teachers using Thinking Maps for their own professional work, they attain a profound transformational stage of development. This transformation not only benefits students but also all educators schoolwide as they see their own thinking continuously improving, just as they promote this vision for their students.

A New Way of Asking and Answering Questions

Throughout the process of creating a Thinking Map, the visual representation of our varied and unique thinking attracts and focuses our attention. We become more consciously aware of the ideas, seeing them now as if for the first time, perhaps. Visually representing our thinking ultimately surfaces ideas in a manner that makes them evident and available to all participants. This deliberate act of picturing individual and collective thoughts and frames of reference increases the likelihood that the group will identify patterns and will make deeper, more meaningful associations.

Our questions themselves become refined, too. Imagine the difference, when confronting an issue, between the starting questions, What do you think about this? and How can we think about this? The first question presumes a clarity that can narrow the thinking and discourse, invite competition, and inhibit the interaction among people needed for the full range of possibilities to emerge. Asking a "how" question elevates the dialogue and recognizes that our thinking patterns create the context in which we make meaning. This entirely different approach signals that we have much to discover and learn before drawing conclusions. It requires suspending judgment, embraces the condition of not knowing, and establishes inquiry as the defining feature of the interaction, reinforcing it as a core value of the organization.

Questions, not answers, offer a genuine starting place for engaging with the complexity of real situations and create the field for collaborative inquiry and decision making. As Judy Morgan from East Syracuse Minoa Central School District states, "We learn through the process of composing questions."

The visual networking of ideas thus literally and figuratively draws people together in the act of collective inquiry and informed decision making. Networking our ideas in response to these questions enlarges, reforms, and reframes those ideas and enriches the field from which we can identify the best possible solutions. As some participants in our study observed, it is as if people in these processes are truly on the same page. As a common visual language for thinking, Thinking Maps implicitly and explicitly place the value of thinking, feeling, and having multiple frames of reference at the heart of the identity and practices of the school. Through the visual communication and construction of ideas, a shared landscape of learning develops—one that the involvement of all members continually nurtures and the bond of this common language strengthens.

Five Common Themes

While the settings of our case studies vary, five common themes connect the stories we'll explore.

1. **Clarity:** Connections drawn individually and collectively with a common language in hand

2. **Efficiency:** Communication that promotes and engages deep thinking

3. **Collaboration:** Engagement through a common language for thinking on the often hazardous journey of problem solving and decision making

4. **Empowerment:** Affirmation of the power of the group and the individuals within it, not from positional power, but from the latent power of their ideas

5. **Sustainability:** Constant dialogue across members of a learning organization as a prerequisite to viable, sustainable, and organizational growth over the long term

Often stated emphatically as well as explicitly, these themes seem to comprise the ground on which the leaders we spoke with built their practice. Each theme represents a critical dimension of connective leadership. As former New York Superintendent Veronica McDermott expresses:

> *[Thinking Maps] opened up the white space that I believe is needed in an organization for real dialogue to occur. I know they enable me to slowly shift from the go-to-guy with the answers to the let's-explore-this together instigator . . . to elicit deep questions and to provoke discussions.*

What she discovered in the process, Veronica observed, "was the latent strengths of the individuals I worked with and the combined power of the group."

Veronica's comments crystallize and encapsulate the themes evidenced in our case studies and in the personal and professional stories that unfold as people within learning organizations explicitly connect the dots—connecting the neural networks in their minds with the visual mapping common patterns of thinking (figure 1.2).

Thinking Maps in Action

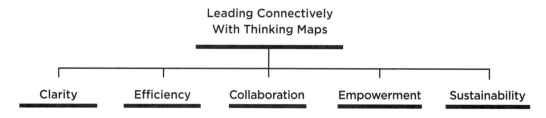

Figure 1.2: Sample Tree Map for the five common themes in connective leadership.

What is different about having a visual representation, and what is its added value? Let's explore a common theme and focus of a leadership team in most every school: student performance.

Let's say, for example, in a discussion within a leadership team, the group is investigating, questioning, and discussing the following questions: What is causing low performance? What are its effects in the school? How do we shift performance to a higher level? This leads to a verbal go-round discussion of possible interventions and ideas about predicted outcomes from each option. Low performance is not a simple problem, and finding solutions requires a complex level of analysis, study, and creative thinking. So the group begins to have a more in-depth conversation, maybe even jotting down a list of causal factors. The members talk about the implications for the culture of the school. They soon begin to consider solutions with identified outcomes. Some of the solutions may be short term; others may be long term with implications across various stakeholder groups. Then, all of a sudden, the group or some members of the group become overwhelmed by the enormity of the problem and even more overwhelmed by the types of differentiated, interdependent thinking required to tackle this problem.

Time also becomes a stressor, one that influences group members to make quick decisions. Some may mention that they only have five minutes more before they have to get back to class or to another meeting. At the same time, many of the participants in the group may be frozen in their seats because of the cognitive load of all the information being discussed and the emotional load of navigating and facing the low performance that the leadership team itself has been responsible for improving. Cognitively and emotionally, we human beings have a very hard time holding onto lots of bits of information, especially different kinds of information framed by personal and professional opinions, beliefs, and strongly held philosophical stances, and most importantly, information being surfaced in settings in which our own performance is part of the discussion.

Of course, the group has designated someone as the note taker and someone else to list ideas on chart paper—all in an effort to capture the fast-moving dialogue driven by multiple voices and backed by roles within the power structure of the school.

The challenge with this kind of common problem-solving situation that leaders face is that the problem itself *is not linear in form*—it is a complex, nonlinear problem framed by emotions and constrained by time. Yet the problem and the multiple influences are usually represented in a linear form during such discussions.

Following is an expanded Multi-Flow Map (figure 1.3) for cause-effect reasoning and systems thinking that the team could use to map out the problem of low performance.

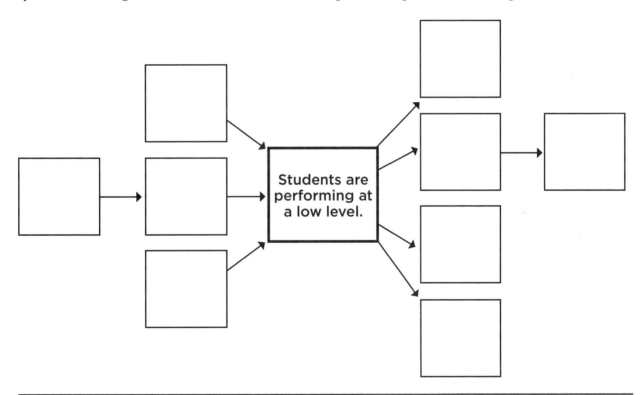

Figure 1.3: Sample expanded Multi-Flow Map to describe low student performance.

As shown in the following maps, participants in this problem-solving context discuss relevant issues of the problem as they would in a normal meeting; they also simultaneously use Thinking Maps to generate, pattern, and reflect on their ideas by expanding the maps and shifting to use different maps according to the kind of thinking they are doing. The *open* maps shown in each case are simply starting points and are provided as examples of how the maps may expand through the group's discussions. Participants would begin with blank pages, flipcharts, whiteboards, or Thinking Maps software to develop, expand, revise, and link together each of the maps. By using the maps, participants have a common visual palette from which to draw out their thinking in patterns that show context, causality, descriptors and attributes, comparisons, and hierarchies that normally would be under-represented in conversations, linear lists, or bullets points.

Before beginning the process, participants in the group would be fluent with the eight different kinds of Thinking Maps (they'll use several of the maps in the course of the process). Though they are asking a seemingly simple question for this particular issue (What are the causes and effects of low performance?), they will ask other questions first to guide and deepen their analysis.

A team involved in a long process of turning around a school in need of improvement needs to define the problem, do a complete analysis, collect data, create solutions, and generate a plan of action and feedback structures. Along the way, team members generate questions (such as, How are we defining low performance in the context of our school?), and as each question arises, they use one or several other maps to connect their ideas. Figure 1.4 shows a sample Circle Map team members might use to explore the characteristics of low performance as they begin their discussion.

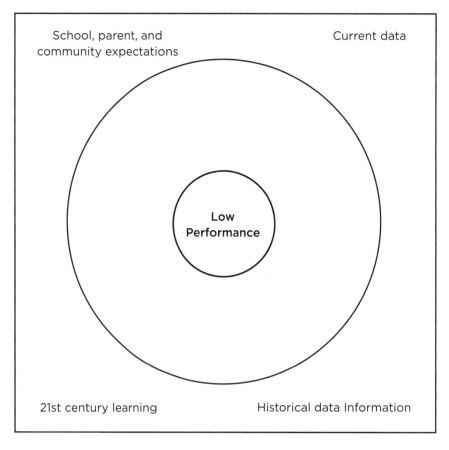

Figure 1.4: Sample Circle Map to describe low student performance.

Next, the team might use a Bubble Map to explore the question, What are the descriptive characteristics of high performance? (See figure 1.5.)

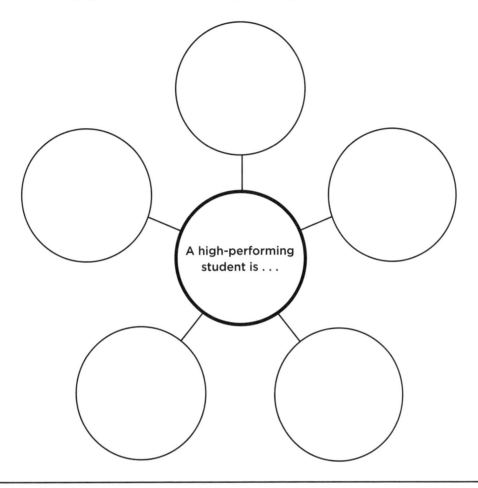

A high-performing student is . . .

Figure 1.5: Sample Bubble Map to describe high student performance.

The team might also ask (and map), "How would we compare and contrast the performance in our school to performance in other schools with similar demographics?" (See figure 1.6, page 14.)

Next, it might ask, "How do we see the different groups of students' performance in content areas?" (See figure 1.7, page 14.)

The team might then look at the school site and explore, What are the physical parts of the school buildings and physical structures in the classroom, and how might this influence performance? (See figure 1.8, page 14.)

The next question might be, For students who perform below expectations, what does the sequence of their days look like, and how does this influence their performance? (See figure 1.9, page 15.)

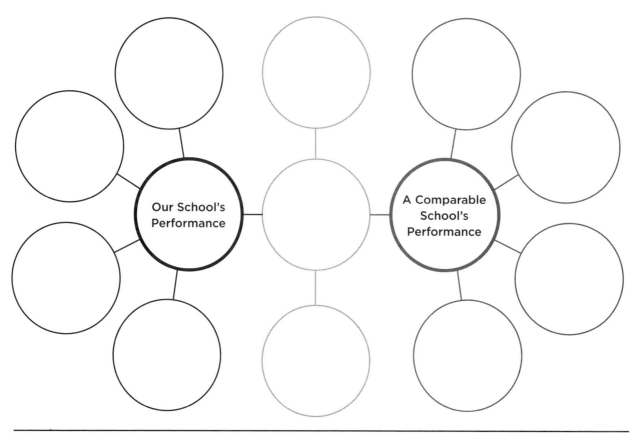

Figure 1.6: Sample Double Bubble Map to compare performance.

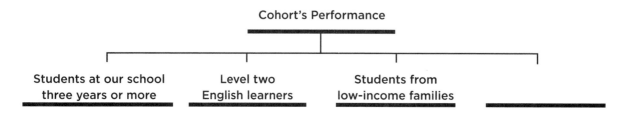

Figure 1.7: Sample Tree Map to describe different students' performance.

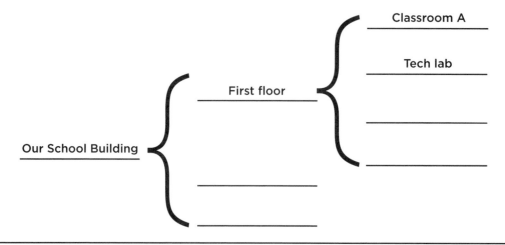

Figure 1.8: Sample Brace Map to describe the school and its influence on performance.

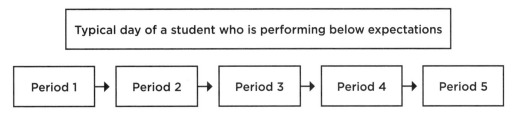

Figure 1.9: Sample Flow Map to describe a day of a low-performing student.

Finally, the team might ask, "What metaphor are we using when we talk to students and each other for representing what we think learning is in the 21st century?" (See figure 1.10.)

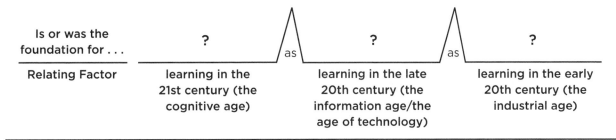

Figure 1.10: Sample Bridge Map to describe learning in the 21st century.

In addition to these questions and the eight maps reflecting the kinds of thinking, the participants would also have become fluent with a *metamap*: the Frame of Reference. Around any of the Thinking Maps, an individual or group may suggest the need to identify the frames of reference that influence the ideas generated in the maps. These *frames* (Lakoff, 1980) are the background belief systems, theories, practical-personal experiences, emotional schemas, and mindsets that drive perceptions and thus deeply influence what is created in each map. Participants simply draw a rectangle around any of the eight maps, and this becomes the *window* of perception. For example, each person in the room discussing the problem of low performance most likely has a professional career that has grown a network of perceptions about what causes low performance. Each person also has a personal story about low performance, either his or her own low performance in school or that of a child or relative. These background experiences along with the existing state in the school in question are often hidden in the recesses of our minds and brains as ghosts. When they surface within the Frame, that capacity for the group to respect the background frames of others leads to clarity, transparency, and a deeper sense of empathy. The *Frame*, as defined in figure 1.1 (page 7), supports thinkers in reflecting on what and how their own personal and professional backgrounds, experiences, values, and beliefs influence their perceptions. The Frame may be used around any of the eight maps. Participants often use it during a problem-solving situation when they realize that the differing opinions and ideas within the group are based on participants' frames of reference, which deeply drive their interpretations.

As described in later chapters through in-depth case studies and analyses, the value of the visual representations and the use of the visual framing of maps in conjunction with verbal conversation lead to greater clarity of ideas and a transparency in seeing other people's ideas.

A Language for Leadership

This brief definition of Thinking Maps as a common visual language—linked to problem solving and connected by essential questions—also helps us see how the maps connect to and are different from the leadership theories, models, and practices discussed in chapter 2. In the field of leadership and systems-change practices—as well as in the realm of classroom teaching, learning, and assessment—umbrella theories, frameworks, and models frame professional development programs and curriculum programs. These programs work to transfer these theories and models by way of supporting strategies, tools, and best practices. For example, Bloom's revised taxonomy of cognitive objectives (Anderson et al., 2001), Senge's five disciplines of systems thinking (Senge, 1990a), Fullan's eight leadership practices (Fullan, 1999), Kotter's eight levels of change (Kotter, 1996), Marzano's nine best practices (Marzano, Pickering, & Pollock, 2001), and Costa's sixteen habits of mind (Costa, 2008a) are each variations of either models or theories grounded in deep research and expressed through programs and supported by proven strategies in the field. Some writing and research, such as Tony Wagner's (2008) work on 21st century learning and leadership, related to innovation and critical thinking are useful as a synthesis and analysis of general directions in the field with broad recommendations for changing the system, a philosophical-political treatise, or both. These writers attempt to define a new paradigm in leadership and bring forth different global concepts or theories about leadership with ideas and techniques for implementation. Some of the research and many if not most of the numerous books on leadership may be defined as conceptual syntheses based on case studies, a range of data, observation, and deeply lived experiences.

Thinking Maps are often used in conjunction with and in support of many of these theories, models, and practices, but the Thinking Maps language is something different. As a language, it is unique and of a different category relative to other effective theory-into-practice innovations. Why are Thinking Maps a *language* and not a model or a theory or simply a collection of practical tools? First, each of the eight maps (and the Frame of Reference) is based on one of eight clearly defined and fundamental cognitive processes. Second, and most importantly, each map has a graphic primitive that represents the process (Double Bubble Map *ovals* for comparisons, Flow Map *boxes* for sequencing, and so on), dynamically expands on use, *and* is combined with the other graphics in much the same way that any language works. Five basic qualities of Thinking Maps that do not pertain to other models or sets of practical tools are shown in figure 1.11.

Each map may expand infinitely, and any and all maps may be linked to and embedded with each other, infinitely leading to a developmental, reflective use of the maps over time.

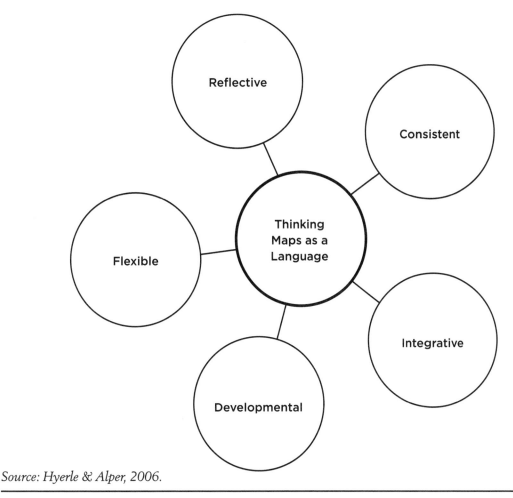

Source: Hyerle & Alper, 2006.

Figure 1.11: Sample Bubble Map for the five basic qualities of Thinking Maps.

This language thus replicates the infinite, complex, and ever-changing dynamism of the neural networks within our brains and the interactions of these networks in social contexts such as schools and workplaces as well as the expanding universe of social networking worldwide.

On first viewing, educators may incorrectly perceive and then define Thinking Maps as a loose collection of graphics (or worse, as static graphic organizers). Those who have learned this language realize that the efficacy of the maps is found in the interdependency between the cognitive processes dynamically and graphically spread across paper, a whiteboard, chart paper, a handheld device, or a computer screen. As reflected in the flow of this book, Thinking Maps are used as a language for individuals, pairs of people, a small group, a whole faculty, and whole school systems. This is possible because of the nature of this language: each box, circle, and line clearly represents a cognitive decision and the act of making meaning.

Thus, Thinking Maps come alive as a language in a learning community by way of the creative act of thinking, learning from oneself and others, and communicating and negotiating meanings in a group of any size. Thinking Maps are easily used to support all theories and models of leadership and learning, because this common language is based in fundamental, if not universal, human cognitive processes such as comparisons, categories, sequences, and causality. These are the unconscious processes of the brain that engage our more conscious minds and frame our interactions and relationships with other people.

The value of Thinking Maps for leadership has been clear from the early stage of Thinking Maps implementation. Even as schools used the maps to support teaching and learning in classrooms, many administrators and teachers also began using the maps for their day-to-day leadership practices. Through these early experiments, we have been inspired to use the maps as a foundation for transformational thinking in every dimension of the school community. The early outcomes from these isolated experiences revealed, as we will discuss, that individuals, leadership teams, and leaders of a school and their board of directors could use this language.

Let's look closely at a school in upstate New York as an example of the direct connection between learning and leading, and then step back and view the implications for Thinking Maps as a language for every participant in a professional learning community, from student to school board director. The director of a school for students with special needs offered us an early powerful example of what can happen when leaders use the maps that their teacher colleagues and students with special needs already use on a day-to-day basis. This story reveals how Thinking Maps can be used for thinking through complex and trying problems for teaching and learning and for communication and leadership. This story also offers a deep and meaningful context for further description of a new language for leading thinking, learning, and communicating in our schools.

We Need a Map!

As the Director of Norman Howard School in Rochester, New York, Marcie Roberts was the central player in an unfolding worst-case scenario. At the end of an eighteen-month time frame during which a schoolwide strategic plan had been built, the plan was now falling apart, and professional relationships were fraying at the edges. Through a well-developed process of working with parents, staff, and board members and bringing in consultants to help craft a new vision for the school, Marcie was faced with the dilemma of so many schools and businesses: their great plan had become a lifeless document they could not follow, and not for lack of trying. The school board members had taken committee positions in order to carry out parts of the strategic plan, but now most board members really could not make sense of the plan; they didn't know exactly what to do or how it fit into the whole vision. They were lost in both the forest (the big-picture vision) and the trees (the practical details and actions). A few said that out of frustration—not disagreement—they were about ready to leave the board.

How could a positive, inclusive, and dynamic process (with committed leaders from both the local business and educational worlds) that produced analyses, strategies, goals, outcomes, and action items dissolve into frustration? Sound familiar? Looking back, Marcie said that after the board approved the plan, it "struggled with what is really a complex and comprehensive strategic plan . . . and it really got unwieldy at the board level. . . . We had two or three very tough, tough meetings where we were getting nowhere."

How many times have you sat alone in your office or felt alone in a meeting with colleagues around you, sensing the disquiet and dissonance of having worked hard to no avail? Have you recognized the complexity of well-formed plans and felt unable to follow through with practical steps? Have you seen plans come cascading slowly down and been unable to do anything about it?

In a breakthrough moment of insight, Marcie responded with the tools that the teachers and the students had been using across their whole school for the past year for improving teaching and learning. (Visit www.thinkingfoundation.org/video/clips/norman-howard-leadership.html to see a video clip of an interview with Marcie Roberts.)

> I thought we need a map, we need a Tree Map. We need to break the plan down into doable portions. I took each of the areas and broke it down into board, staff, board and staff *and interpreted the plan under each area of responsibility. We clarified it with the Tree Map, but we needed to give them a way for them to work with it. That was the hurdle by far. I brought out a Flow Map. (Thinking Foundation, n.d.b)

Marcie visually mapped out the strategic plan using multiple Thinking Maps. She created a PowerPoint presentation with only a few slides (figures 1.12 and 1.13, pages 20–21).

PowerPoint presentations lead millions of meetings every day around the world across organizations, but this *was not* another linear, bulleted show with distracting graphics fading in and out, up-tempo music, and repetitive, often disconnected points. Marcie transformed the dozen-page strategic plan—complex nonlinear ideas lost within the walls of linear text—into an elegant visual synthesis on a few color-coded Thinking Maps. Here were mental roadmaps for all the travelers to follow, uniting them on a common path. The board members were invited to the school theater, and Marcie unveiled the maps. Surfacing with clarity and coherence, the consolidated plan reflected eighteen months of larger school committee work in a vision for the future of the school. After she concluded, as Marcie describes it, the board members were quiet for a moment, and then they rose in the large hall to give her a standing ovation.

Later, as Marcie reflected on this event and the board's refocusing, she said:

> This has meaning now. It has relevance. They have seen it in action; they have seen it used. It showed a way for the work to become more focused; it's ordered. It's discrete. It's got a beginning and it's got an end. It has visible outcomes. It gives people an extremely clear, specific idea of the work. Modeling this work for the board has been phenomenal. The outcome was

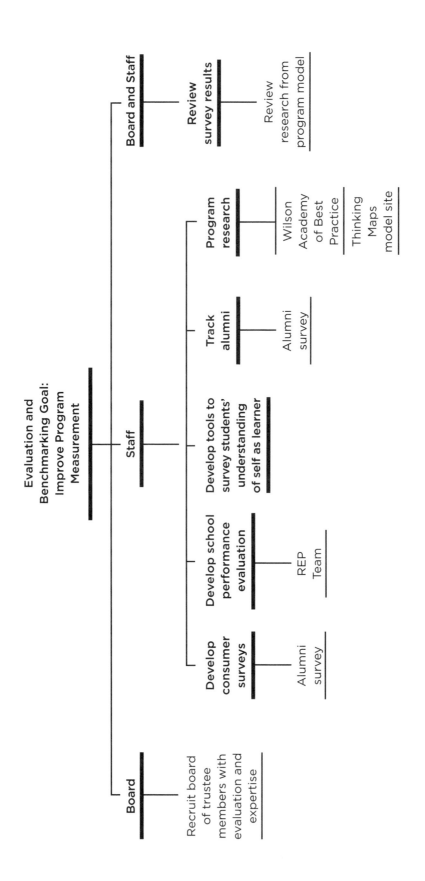

Figure 1.12: Sample Tree Map for the evaluation and benchmarking goal.

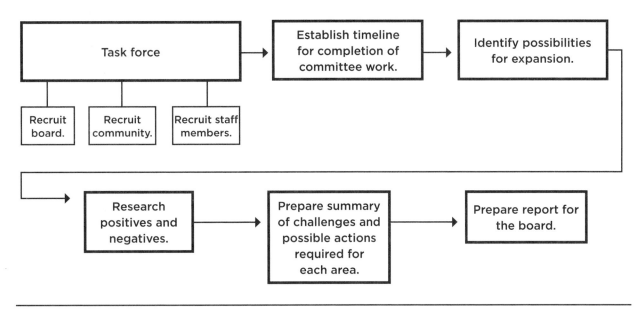

Figure 1.13: Sample Flow Map for the task force responsibilities and procedures.

that we had a training for the board members so they could be proficient in the maps. It clarified everything. Better yet they said that this is a great tool for evaluating your work as the head of the school. (Thinking Foundation, n.d.b)

Marcie stated that one board member admitted later that until the maps had been presented, he had never really understood how all of the complex workings of school fit together. Other board members stated that the fully developed maps helped them see the step-by-step actions they had to take for specific tasks and how the outcomes of their work fit into the bigger picture of the Norman Howard School. They could see the parts *visually connected* to the whole.

This is not just a story of using a few discrete leadership tools; it is a story of effective leadership using Thinking Maps as a language for learning across the school. How? If you walked down the hallway from Marcie's office and entered Mr. K's history classroom, a similar story was playing in parallel with the same qualities and outcomes seen in the boardroom. High school teacher Mr. K (as he is called by teachers and students alike) and his students were using the Thinking Maps to make sense of U.S. history as preparation for the New York State Regents Exam.

Norman Howard School is unique. It is a state-accredited, grades 5–12 school for students with special needs serving forty school districts in the greater Rochester area. Students use Thinking Maps regularly across disciplines for remembering, analyzing, and understanding content concepts (the forest) and content facts and academic vocabulary (the trees). Mr. K describes his experience as follows. (Visit www.thinkingfoundation.org/video /clips/norman-howard-mr-k.html to see a video clip of an interview with Mr. K.)

> *[I was] comfortable with the way I was teaching, but when students came in they had been using it [the maps] in writing, in science. Their buy-in actually helped my buy-in. They were seeing it as an effective tool. By the time I started using the maps my students already had a firm grasp they just jumped in and starting using the maps. I started stealing from them. (Thinking Foundation, n.d.a)*

Though Mr. K had begun training in the maps, his ability to "steal" application ideas from his students shows that the maps are transferable, like any language or high-quality tool set. Marcie was stealing the maps from her teachers for use with the board, and the board members then saw how they could amplify the use of the tools for evaluating her performance. Mr. K used Thinking Maps in his practice of teaching and realized that he could use the maps that each student generated as dynamic formative assessment tools. Mr. K deepened his explanation:

> *I use them for assessment of their knowledge but also of my teaching. What they pick up is maybe not what I wanted them to pick up. I will be able to cover the material more quickly, more efficiently, and really help the students to focus in on the key points. The Thinking Maps really highlight the key points. Truthfully, it helps me focus. I want them to look down at a map and say hey, that really makes sense to me. (Thinking Foundation, n.d.a)*

Stepping back from this experience, we see in explicit terms the vision of the use of Thinking Maps as a common visual language for leadership and learning at every level of the school community. The director of a school, answerable to a school board with a strategic plan, used the same language as the high school teachers, answerable to a classroom full of students, many struggling with textbooks and concepts across disciplines. The struggle for all is knowing how to deal with an overwhelming amount of complex, comprehensive, and interrelated information and texts that often do not offer clarity or make sense. Marcie, the school board, Mr. K, and students all used an adaptive language for supporting their respective groups in *making meaning* from a wash of information and for transforming lifeless documents and information into relevant, meaningful, and actionable knowledge.

A Language for Connective Knowing

What does thinking look like? This may strike most educators as an odd question. Most often we perceive thinking as hidden in the brain and mind behind the interior monologue of our moment-to-moment thoughts and dreams, the words we use to communicate our thoughts to others, the papers we write, the emails we send off, and the mathematical problems we solve. We squeeze our words out in strings of sentences like toothpaste from a tube, but we know deep down that our thoughts and concepts are underrepresented by words alone. Even a picture that says a thousand words doesn't do justice to the complexity of our ideas. As we discovered through the story of Norman Howard School, the well-meaning and collaborative participants in a strategic planning process could not *see* their thinking nor transform their actions accordingly until Marcie Roberts mapped them out using Thinking Maps.

Defining the context and frame of reference for this transitional point in the history of our educational systems nationally and globally is essential for understanding how Thinking Maps offer a new language for communication and improvement of thinking, learning, and leading. Leaders in the field of education, parents, businesspeople, and students as future innovators in a global network of technologies and knowledge workers are asking for a new way to facilitate learning and co-leadership in the collaborative work structures of the 21st century.

At first blush, the concept of Thinking Maps may look all too simple, and that is good because as it turns out, simplicity is an essential quality of the maps. The capacity to think, reflect, and then transform our thinking into new behaviors and actions is foundational to living in this new century of connective technology, global knowledge creation, and knowledge transfer. As we shall investigate in the stories to follow, through their seeming simplicity, Thinking Maps can animate high-quality thinking and nurture self-reflection, metacognition, and dynamic reflective leadership within groups of people. The essential and unique human quality of empathy grows ever more present when we have a language for connecting our thoughts.

In the next chapter, we will introduce the five thematic strands that emerged from our research (clarity, efficiency, collaboration, empowerment, and sustainability). Following an explanation of each theme as we understood it from our study, a brief survey of some of the literature in the field will place our research in the context of other important work in the field. This merging of theory and practice is an essential component and constant challenge for those working as leaders in the field of education. Ultimately, however, what allows our actions to be aligned with our beliefs makes them more purposeful and effective.

Thematic Strands in the Literature on Effective Leadership: The Roots of Connectivity

The soul cannot think without a picture.

—ARISTOTLE

If you can't imagine it, you can never do it. In my experience, the image always precedes the reality.

—MARILYN KING

School leaders have tremendous influence over the degree to which their schools and the individuals within them act intelligently and effectively. Influential leaders understand the fundamental nature of learning not only as it relates to students but as an essential dimension of the dynamics of the school community itself. With a vision of what it means for a school to be a learning community, they work thoughtfully and skillfully to bring others into this vision and develop their capacities to contribute in positive and constructive ways.

It is imperative that effective school leaders create effective schools for students. Few, if any, poorly led schools have been able to achieve or sustain high levels of student performance. With ever-growing demands on school leaders—and a shrinking pool of well-prepared leaders, or individuals who are too inexperienced to effectively lead—preparing our future and current school leaders for the challenges that they will (and do) face is essential now more than ever. However, what makes effective school leaders, and how do we best prepare them for the complexity they face? How do they develop as civil engineers capable of designing the infrastructures—the pathways, bridges, and networks—necessary to ensure meaningful and productive interactions among people and universal access to information and ideas?

These questions have challenged educators and researchers for decades. Recent research presented in this chapter—including wide-scale studies, meta-analyses of thousands of studies conducted over decades, and intensive case studies of effective leaders—has shed some light on these questions.

Emergent Leadership Themes

The five themes that our research shows are associated with the effective use of Thinking Maps for leadership—(1) clarity, (2) efficiency, (3) collaboration, (4) empowerment, and (5) sustainability (see the Multi-Flow Map in figure 2.1)—are also evident throughout the literature on leadership and expressed in a variety of ways. However, leaders in our study reported that using Thinking Maps gave these themes added meaning.

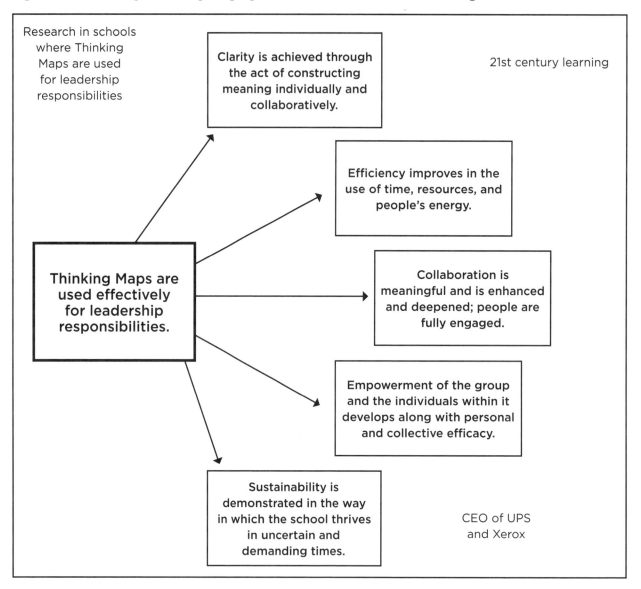

Figure 2.1: Sample Multi-Flow Map for the five themes of leadership with sources and several influencing elements cited in the Frame of Reference.

Clarity, as we came to understand it through the comments of the leaders we interviewed, is not the presumptive certainty of one's opinions but something that develops from a satisfying process of constructing meaning alone and in concert with others; from suspending judgment and engaging in a process of individual and collective dialogue in order to allow patterns to emerge. These internal and external conversations were facilitated by a visual language that made evident the content of the ideas, the processes used to arrive at them, and the frames of reference that influenced them. Clarity, too, came from knowing that the actions one decided on aligned with core values and beliefs.

Efficiency, we learned from our research, was not to be confused with *expediency*. Certainly, time was an influencing factor in all of the scenarios leaders discussed with us. However, the stress occurred not so much from having too little time but rather from being aware that they could not use their time as effectively as they believed they should. Having more time does not necessarily guarantee that it will be used well. In inefficiently led meetings or in personal processing that gets bogged down, frustration develops not from running out of time but from using that time inefficiently—something more time wouldn't solve. With Thinking Maps, leaders reported that people were more focused and deeply engaged, their attention was more sharply directed, their thinking was attuned, and their ability to do what the brain strives to do—*see and construct patterns*—was supported. The leaders felt the resulting decisions and the actions that developed had integrity and were not simply made to "get it done."

Collaboration was certainly identified in our research as both an essential aspect of learning communities and an area in which the use of Thinking Maps contributed positively in significant ways. However, as Michael Fullan observes, "Collaborative cultures, which by definition have close relationships, are indeed powerful, but unless they are focusing on the right thing, they may end up being powerfully wrong" (Fullan, 2001a, p. 67). The collaboration that school leaders spoke of in our research was not simply the act of bringing people together, but of grounding the collaborative process of learning in which participants were engaged at all levels—intellectually, emotionally, morally, politically, and so on.

In the context of collaboration, dispositions such as intellectual curiosity, commitment to understanding, and suspension of judgment—striving for clarity—were essential elements of the process of working together. While Thinking Maps were a vehicle for bringing people together, they also served to focus the attention of the group on the ideas and not each other. The collaborative process, while social in nature, became highly purposeful and insistent on achieving clarity.

As is now perhaps becoming apparent, the interplay of these themes is, in itself, a crucial observation about the influence Thinking Maps had on these school communities. The collaborative processes described and the clarity and efficiency with which people arrived at understandings individually and collectively could not have been achieved at the levels reported to us if people didn't feel empowered to contribute their ideas to these important processes in their school communities. *Empowerment* not only was experienced and exercised as a right of those participating in a democratic context, but it emerged from the confidence gained through using the maps in the ability to formulate and communicate one's thinking and clarify one's ideas internally and to others. The internal web of the school community operated at its highest degree of efficiency and effectiveness when all members of the school were fully engaged, affirmed, and able to confidently engage in situations in which answers and solutions were not immediately apparent.

It's not surprising that we would reserve *sustainability* for last. We learned that the leaders were not simply speaking about maintaining some sort of status quo or holding precious what their schools had become. Instead, the sustainability they referred to and reached for was the dynamic state of learning—the constant process of being built up and sustained by a common visual language for thinking. This common language expressed a core value of these schools—that thinking is the foundation for all learning at all levels throughout their school communities. Eleanor Duckworth, educator and author, once wrote that it is virtuous not to know. It's what we do when we don't know that will ultimately determine what we do know (Duckworth, 2006). In the 21st century, where change is the norm, thinking schools will embrace the opportunities that present themselves, adapt to new circumstances, and create their own futures, as Senge (1990a) proposes healthy organizations will do. Sustainability, then, is about not simply surviving in these dynamic and uncertain times but thriving with the benefit of the clarity, efficiency, collaboration, and empowerment that leading connectively through the use of Thinking Maps can inspire.

Research on Effective School Leaders

Leithwood, Seashore Louis, Anderson, and Wahlstrom (2004) describe three qualities of effective leaders based on their research.

1. **Effective leaders are good at helping people develop their full potential:** They create situations that enable teachers and others to do their jobs successfully, offer intellectual support to improve the work, and serve as role models of practice and support.

2. **Effective leaders can set direction for the organization:** They set trends through developing shared goals, monitoring organizational performance, and promoting good communication.

3. **Effective leaders can redesign their organizations as needed:** They create a productive school culture, change or remove obstacles such as organizational structures that make work difficult, and work collaboratively and to build collaborative processes.

School leaders have the power and potential to transform an organization. However, to be effective and connective, leaders must not only have a vision for the organization, but they must also work effectively and collaboratively with others to make positive changes. In their overview of the literature on school leaders, Davis, Darling-Hammond, LaPoint, and Meyerson (2005) suggest current research has focused on three primary practices:

1. Supporting teachers and understanding the work they do

2. Focusing on student learning through management of the curriculum and other strategies that empower students

3. Transforming organizations into more effective places focused on improving teaching and learning for all students

This notion of *transforming* is highlighted in the following discussion of the research on effective leaders—as is the support of teachers with the ultimate focus on student learning. Connective leadership supports the work of all people in the school—including teachers and students—keeping the focus on student learning. The use of the Thinking Maps maintains the focus on the inextricable connection between cognition and learning not only for students but for all learners (teachers, administrators, and others) in a school community.

Create a Balanced Leadership Framework

In their comprehensive meta-analysis on leadership, Marzano, Waters, and McNulty (2005) create a balanced leadership framework in which they describe the knowledge, skills, strategies, resources, and tools educational leaders need to improve student achievement. The premise of the framework is that effective leadership means more than simply knowing what to do; it means knowing when, how, and why to do it. The authors claim that sufficient research supports the connection between student achievement and effective leadership in both directions—that is, ineffective leaders are associated with reductions in student achievement, and effective leaders are related to increased student achievement.

The Marzano et al. (2005) model uses the effect sizes from the meta-analysis to show that the following twenty-one leadership qualities have an impact on student learning. The leader:

1. Fosters shared beliefs and a sense of community and cooperation

2. Establishes a set of standard operating procedures and routines

3. Protects teachers from issues and influences that would detract from their teaching time and focus

4. Provides teachers with materials and professional development necessary for the successful execution of their jobs

5. Is directly involved in the design and implementation of curriculum, instruction, and assessment practices

6. Establishes clear goals and keeps those goals in the forefront of the school's attention

7. Is knowledgeable about current curriculum, instruction, and assessment practices

8. Has quality contact and interactions with teachers and students

9. Recognizes and rewards individual accomplishments

10. Establishes strong lines of communication with teachers and among students

11. Is an advocate and spokesperson for the school to all stakeholders

12. Involves teachers in the design and implementation of important decisions and policies

13. Recognizes and celebrates school accomplishments and acknowledges failures

14. Demonstrates an awareness of the personal aspects of teachers and staff

15. Is willing to and actively challenges the status quo

16. Inspires and leads new and challenging innovations

17. Communicates and operates from strong ideals and beliefs about schooling

18. Monitors the effectiveness of school practices and their impact on student learning

19. Adapts leadership behaviors to the needs of the current situation and is comfortable with dissent

20. Is aware of the details and undercurrents in the running of the school and uses this information to address current and potential problems

21. Ensures that faculty and staff are aware of the most current theories and practices and makes the discussion of these a regular aspect of the school culture

The authors of this study also discuss four types of knowledge that one can use when engaging the twenty-one leadership responsibilities and practices (see figure 2.2). These four areas can be useful for teachers and administrators as they think about their role as leaders and the knowledge that is needed to lead. In our experience with the school leaders profiled throughout this book, their use of the Thinking Maps influenced their knowledge in each of these four important areas. We have provided several examples of leaders using the maps to guide their quest through muddy waters to discern what is important, what to do, and how and when to do it.

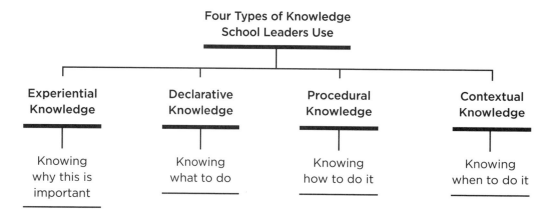

Figure 2.2: Sample Tree Map for the four types of knowledge.

Clearly Define and Understand the Leadership Role

Davis et al. (2005) conducted an intensive research study of effective leaders along with a comprehensive review of the research literature on school leadership. They found that:

> Principals play a vital and multifaceted role in setting the direction for schools that are positive and productive workplaces for teachers and vibrant learning environments for children, but existing knowledge on the best ways to develop these effective leaders is insufficient.

In this study, Christine LeVita, former president of the Wallace Foundation, makes the case for the critically important role of school leadership and improving our understanding of strategies that work to improve school leadership. She writes:

> More than ever, in today's climate of heightened expectations, principals are in the hot seat to improve teaching and learning. They need to be educational visionaries, instructional and curriculum leaders, assessment experts, disciplinarians, community builders, public relations experts, budget analysts, facility managers, special programs administrators, and expert overseers of legal, contractual, and policy mandates and initiatives. They are expected to broker the often-conflicting interests of parents, teachers, students, district office officials, unions, and state and federal agencies, and they need to be sensitive to the widening range of student needs. (as cited in Davis et al., 2005, p. 1)

Davis and his colleagues (2005) cite key findings from their intensive research of successful school leaders. First, they identify the programs that have demonstrated success in preparing successful school leaders to "influence student achievement through two important pathways—the support and development of effective teachers and the implementation of effective organizational processes" (p. 1).

Their second key finding is that successful programs for developing, educating, and preparing school leaders have essential components. These programs are "research-based, have curricular coherence, provide experience in authentic contexts, use cohort groupings and mentors, and are structured to enable collaborative activity between the program and area schools" (p. 2).

Their third key finding is that one can take different paths to become a successful leader—different combinations of experience, theory, and academic preparation.

Integrate Four Leadership Frames

Bolman and Deal (1997), in their theoretical framework for leaders in *Reframing Organizations*, describe four kinds of key leadership frames: (1) structural, (2) human resources, (3) political, and (4) symbolic (table 2.1, page 32). They suggest that successful leaders integrate these four frames.

Table 2.1: Four Key Leadership Frames

	Effective Leadership		Ineffective Leadership	
Frame	Leader	Leadership Process	Leader	Leadership Process
Structural	Analyst, architect	Analysis, design	Petty tyrant	Management by detail and fiat
Human Resources	Catalyst, servant	Support, empowerment	Weakling, pushover	Abdication
Political	Advocate, negotiator	Advocacy, coalition building	Con artist, thug	Manipulation, fraud
Symbolic	Prophet, poet	Inspiration, framing experience	Fanatic, fool	Mirage, smoke and mirrors

Source: Adapted from Bolman & Deal, 1997.

The structural frame contains specialized tasks, sequential work, close supervision, and tendencies to work from the top down. In this frame, goals and objectives are paramount, and the rational steps are prioritized over personal beliefs. Its focus is efficiency and specialization. In the human resources frame, leaders create an open system where good and bad news are shared up and down the hierarchy, and the focus is on individual workers' skills and trying to create productive organizations. Leaders focus on meeting the hierarchy of needs of the workers (physiological, safety, belongingness, esteem, and self-actualization). In the political frame, issues of power, conflict, tactics, and authority are considered. Leaders are expected to be constructive politicians. They are able to map the political terrain, network, build coalitions, bargain, and negotiate. In the symbolic frame, leaders seek to create organizations that have a group identity and shared sense of history. They lead by example and use humor and play to encourage creativity.

Build Leadership Capacity

Linda Lambert has written extensively on the topic of educational leadership—how to develop effective leaders, build leadership capacity, and sustain the progress of leaders. She asks us to rethink how we construct leadership, arguing that "we can view leadership as a verb, rather than a noun, by considering the processes, activities and relationships in which people engage, rather than as the individual in a specific role" (Lambert, 1998, p. 2). She argues further that we should think about constructivist leadership as "learning among adults in a community that shares goals and visions" (p. 2). She further argues that for this way of thinking to work, we must make the following assumptions:

- *Leadership* and *leader* are not synonymous—leaders do leadership work.
- Leadership should be about creating positive, constructive change through learning.
- Leadership is something that anybody can and should be allowed and encouraged to do.
- Leadership is shared and works toward creating democratic schools.
- Leadership shares power and voice of authority and works toward shared learning.

In her model of leadership and building capacity for leadership, the act of leading is shared, and professionals are encouraged to be involved. Among her advice to those wishing to build capacity for effective leaders are the following (Lambert, 1998, p. 19):

1. *Hire personnel with the proven capacity to do leadership work and develop veteran staff to become skillful leaders.*

2. *Get to know one another; build trusting relationships.*

3. *Assess staff and school capacity for leadership. Do you have a shared purpose? Do you work collaboratively? Is there a schoolwide focus on student achievement and adult learning?*

4. *Develop a culture of inquiry that includes a continuous cycle of reflecting, questioning, gathering evidence, and planning for improvement.*

5. *Organize for leadership work by establishing inclusive governance structures and collaborative inquiry processes.*

6. *Implement plans for building leadership capacity—and anticipate role changes and professional development needs.*

7. *Develop district policies and practices that support leadership capacity building. These practices include district-school relationships built on high engagement but few rules and regulations, as well as shared decision making and site-based school management. Districts should model the processes of a learning organization.*

Embrace and Engage Diversity

An important quality of today's connective leaders is the ability to embrace and engage diversity. Wasserman and Gallegos (2007) encourage leaders to use the REAL model to engage diversity and use "disorienting dilemmas to transform relationships" (p. 3). The REAL model proposes the following strategies for leaders to consider to strengthen the effectiveness of their organization through "destabilizing entrenched habits and exploring new, more creative paths of engaging" (Wasserman & Gallegos, 2007, p. 3). (See figure 2.3, page 34.)

As the authors claim:

> *Leveraging the value of diversity requires fostering a culture of inclusion to develop the skills and competencies that cannot be easily transmitted in a short training session. Advancing an inclusive culture requires new skills that call for shifting habits of mind and habits of relating. (Wasserman & Gallegos, 2007, p. 6)*

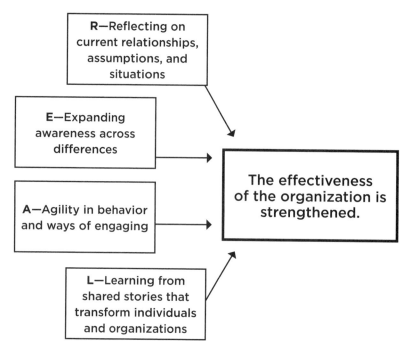

Source: Adapted from Wasserman & Gallegos, 2007, pp. 3–5.

Figure 2.3: Sample Multi-Flow Map of the REAL model.

Certainly, leaders committed to organizational improvement and change within our increasingly diverse workforce must consider strategies to shift our more traditional ways of thinking and collaborating and create more inclusive environments.

Excel in the Five Disciplines of Organizational Change

In *The Fifth Discipline*, Senge (1990a) discusses the notion of learning organizations and posits his own theoretical framework of organizational change and leadership that draws from his prior work in systems thinking as well as collaborative processes and team building. He identifies five disciplines of organizational change: (1) systems thinking, (2) personal mastery, (3) mental models, (4) shared vision, and (5) team learning. He proposes that these "might just as well be called leadership disciplines as the learning disciplines. Those who excel in these areas will be the natural leaders of learning organizations" (Senge, 1990a, p. 3). He defines a learning organization as allowing people to "continually expand their capacity to create the results they truly desire, where new and expansive patterns of thinking are nurtured, where collective aspiration is set free, and where people are continually learning to see the whole together" (p. 4). These organizations, he contends, are more likely to adapt and consequently be more productive. Such organizations require a particular kind of leadership that is clearly aligned with the five disciplines of organizational change.

Senge argues that long-term change within organizations is difficult (as cited in Saposnick, 2000). Despite the fact that most people think that a single powerful leader can make significant and lasting changes, the truth is that because of the complexities of most educational organizations, no single leader can accomplish this alone. However, the picture isn't that bleak. Senge states that long-term sustainable change is possible, even in very complex organizations, "when lots of people at all levels of an organization start to do things differently" (as cited in Saposnick, 2000, p. 2). Sustaining change in bureaucratic organizations is complex and challenging, but not impossible if we are able to get many people doing things differently. As we will see, when Thinking Maps are used as a language throughout the school and at the leadership level, true and sustainable improvements happen.

Sustain Successful Leadership

Once we determine what makes, creates, and defines successful leadership, the next imperative is to sustain successful leadership. In their article "Sustaining Leadership," Hargreaves and Fink (2003) write, "Educational change is rarely easy to make, always hard to justify and almost impossible to sustain" (p. 1). They argue further that all too often, reformers conflate the notion of sustainability with *maintainability*—simply making a change *last* rather than sustaining the *impact* of the change. Grounded in their study of a five-year program in Ontario and in New York high schools, the authors arrive at the following conclusions. First, our notions of leadership should be "embedded in the hearts and minds of the many and not rest on the shoulders of an heroic few" (Hargreaves & Fink, 2003, p. 16). Second, "educational systems should see leadership as a vertical system over time" (p. 16) rather than a series of different leaders—leaders should see how they fit within the series of previous leaders and the changes they have made. Leaders should be seen as an asset rather than a cost. Finally, "the promise of sustainable success in education lies in creating cultures of distributed leadership throughout the school community, not in training and developing a tiny leadership elite" (p. 17). This notion of distributed leadership is essential to their framework. This does not mean that leaders simply do more delegation, but they create leadership opportunities for many others—to provide a depth of leadership in the organization that will help sustain changes.

Broaden the Scope of Leadership and Contemplate Human Purpose

Based on their work with over 150 leaders in science, business, education, and other fields, Peter Senge and his colleagues Scharmer, Jaworski, and Flowers (2004) sought to better understand how "profound collective change occurs" (as cited in Hall, 2005, p. 1). George Hall conducted a compelling interview with Senge and Scharmer about their book *Presence: Human Purpose and the Field of the Future* to gather their thoughts on organizational learning, among other themes (Hall, 2005). Comments from this interview show the importance of universal strategies as well as some of the ways leaders tend to approach organizational change. Scharmer argues:

> *Many entrepreneurs and founders of successful companies have developed a special capacity to sense an emerging reality. When they tapped into the*

emerging reality and sensed their next opportunity, they tapped into a different sort of knowing within themselves. They felt this opportunity that they then tried to realize. I knew that this type of innovation, which the economist Brian Arthur writes about, could be captured in a model. We developed such a model—the Theory of the U. This model describes this capacity to innovate as one U-shaped process with three highly nuanced stages. First, you open up to and immerse yourself into your context. In Arthur's words, you "observe, observe, and observe." Second, you retreat out of this total immersion. You retreat and reflect deeply and allow an inner knowing to emerge of its own accord. While engaging in a state of deep reflection, a spark or an idea will begin to emerge from that process. Then, in the third phase, you move that spark into reality by practical experimentation and prototyping, which involves taking action and learning by doing quickly. (as cited in Hall, 2005, p. 2)

Leaders in education need tools and support to engage in this kind of process that Senge and Scharmer describe. Connective leaders seemed to engage in similar processes with the Thinking Maps to facilitate, as will be described more thoroughly in the case studies within the book.

Several notions from this interview will be covered later in this book. The first is the notion of universal ways of thinking. In their proposed Theory of the U, Senge and Scharmer argue that this strategy is universal across cultures for innovators. The eight Thinking Maps share this cognitive universality. Second, they discuss the notion of observing and seeing what was not there before. Language of *images* and *pictures* is pervasive in the leadership literature. Leaders must be able to *see* the often-called bigger picture and think about how to improve it.

Human Capacity

Among the common themes across the research we've discussed so far is the reliance on the intelligent, thoughtful behavior not only of the designated or titled leader of the school but of all within it in order to fulfill the school's mission. There is an implicit and explicit connection between leading and learning; put another way, the leader leads the learning for all members of the school community. Leadership and learning are inextricably linked. The capacity of human beings to learn, grow, and develop insight and understanding represents perhaps the greatest opportunity for schools to achieve success. Michael Dickmann and Nancy Stanford-Blair (2002) put forward the challenge this way: "Leaders at the beginning of this new millennium must seize the moment and become mindful practitioners, leaders who are stewards of organizational intelligence" (p. 133). With that stewardship comes the responsibility to nurture the ability in others to act and think intelligently and maximize one of the most important capacities human beings possess—the ability to learn.

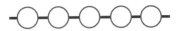

Effective, connective leadership works to create effective, connective schools capable of developing successful students who will become our next generation of workers and leaders in the global marketplace and will lead fulfilling and productive lives. In the ensuing chapters, we further develop the concepts of connective knowing and leading. We present individual and collective acts of leadership supported by the use of Thinking Maps and examine them through the thematic lenses of clarity, efficiency, collaboration, empowerment, and sustainability. From these accounts, Thinking Maps emerge as a shared visual language for leading and learning, a language that is naturally attuned to the human brain, aligned with our inherent motivation to know and understand, and ideally suited for engineering the connectivity needed to address the complex challenges of education in the 21st century.

Leaders as Teachers: Facilitating Individual Learning, Growth, and Development

Many view the quality of relationships in an organization as the foundation for its accomplishments and success. In schools, as in other organizational settings, the culture that develops as an expression of these dynamics is a central determining factor of the school's ability to improve and thrive. Bolman and Deal (1997) identify culture as one of the "wellsprings of high performance" in high-performing groups (p. 261). Martin-Kniep (2008) cites research suggesting that culture can create the conditions for people to act courageously and exercise initiative without fear of retribution or ridicule. Wagner et al. (2006) define culture as "the shared values, beliefs, assumptions, expectations, and behaviors related to students and learning, teachers and teaching, instructional leadership, and the quality of relationships within and beyond school" (p. 102). Culture, they say, represents the "invisible and powerful meanings and mindsets held individually and collectively throughout the system" (p. 102).

The culture of a school has an impact on the development of individuals within it and the system as a whole. The degree to which individuals will take risks, for example, can be enhanced or inhibited by the nature of the support and encouragement they receive from their colleagues as well as those in leadership positions. The same is true for the school as a whole, whose overall development can be viewed as a consequence of the presence or lack of support for the individuals within it. A school's culture, when infected by competition, lack of respect, and isolation, can impede learning at the adult level as well as the student level.

Goleman, Boyatzis, and McKee (2002) suggest that the culture of an organization can take on the consistency of "a kind of emotional soup" in which everyone contributes a bit of his or her own personal spice (p. 8). Great potential occurs in organizations for a rich interplay of ideas and emotions, a network of information, and the emergence of shared meanings and individual and collective insights. However, they note, the leader "adds the strongest seasoning" (p. 8). Those in positions of responsibility, authority, or formal leadership roles experience this acutely. They understand that while everyone contributes to the conversation, their contributions carry additional weight and meaning—sometimes not necessarily intended or desired. Their words and actions send powerful signals to people within and across the system. They can sweeten the pot or leave a bitter taste.

Peter Senge states, "The word *organization* [italics added] is a product of how we think and how we act; (it) cannot change in a fundamental way unless we change our basic patterns of thinking and acting" (as cited in Galagan, 1991, p. 39). This is equally true in interpersonal settings and in groups. The nature of a leader's relationships with others also reflects underlying core values and beliefs. These beliefs and values are made evident through the choices made during an interaction—how people are seated in relationship to each other—for example, whether or not an inquiry approach is used—and the particular words and phrases chosen that signal attitudes and reveal intentions. Relationships develop from engagement and the specific actions—words, gestures, postures, and so on—used in the course of the interactions. These actions are highly suggestive of, if not directly evident of, particular values and beliefs the leader held. They can communicate a sense of safety and an invitation to engage or a warning to retreat and withdraw. Congruency between actions and beliefs is critical to establishing trust in relationships. Gardner (1995) states, "It is important for leaders to know their stories, to get them straight, to communicate them effectively, and, above all, to embody in their lives the stories that they tell" (p. xi).

While not necessarily preordained, the relationships we form are, however, often influenced by attitudes and expectations associated with powerful factors like role, gender, and history. These forces represent our frame of reference—the accumulation of key experiences, personal and professional, that anchor our lives. From these experiences, we make predictions and, consequently, decisions about new events. The patterns formed and fixed in our frame become a powerful filter through which new experiences flow and are interpreted. They prepare us for the next events, sometimes with openness and heightened anticipation and other times with anxiety or dread. They are critical to our survival and happiness and therefore difficult to overcome and easy to reinforce. This filter can be reassuring and affirming, or it can be inhibiting—one reason why relationships in general and those involving power and authority in particular are so complicated. In this realm, we found the use of Thinking Maps yielded significant benefit to both leaders and those in relationships with them.

Throughout our research, we saw many examples of school leaders—superintendents, principals, and coaches—using Thinking Maps with resounding success in very delicate situations with teachers. In some instances, the situations had escalated to include union officials and grievance personnel. All situations involved professional content, yet all were deeply personal. In these situations, the challenge involved acknowledging the highly personal nature of these professional interactions and the vulnerability and discomfort that often accompany such experiences and transforming the interaction into more than its apparent destiny. Senge (1990a) notes, "Leaders as teachers help people restructure their views of reality . . . and therefore see new possibilities for shaping the future" (p. 12). The following case studies all had different outcomes, but the process of using Thinking Maps provided clarity, reduced negative emotions, and resulted in a path that was best for all and allowed each leader to use his or her position instructively and constructively.

Walking the Talk

We know the story all too well: parents and students complain about a teacher, accusations are made, and while people have raised such issues before, nothing documented in past performance evaluations and no concrete evidence in personnel files indicate any problems that needed attention. Immediately, the teacher feels threatened, the principal is under pressure to act, the union responds to ensure an appropriate process is followed, and the superintendent is called on to intervene, while the issue agitates school board members.

In Superintendent Michael Sampson's case, however, by the time the issue reached him, communication between the teacher and the principal had broken down completely. Feeling threatened, the teacher had already filed a formal grievance with the union. Emotions were running high, and restoring communication on their own was beyond the reach of the teacher and principal. Fortunately for Michael, he had cultivated trusting relationships throughout the system, and most, if not all, viewed his involvement as a positive and hopeful step. Nonetheless, the conflict seemed intractable, with all parties rooted in their beliefs and emotions, and headed for arbitration.

Although relatively new to this district, Michael had successfully begun the process of establishing a strong reputation as a solid instructional leader. He introduced Thinking Maps throughout the system, something he had done successfully in his previous district as the assistant superintendent for curriculum and instruction. Michael extended the introduction of Thinking Maps beyond the classroom to include members of the district's leadership team. He used the maps in his own practice, facilitating meetings and communicating information to others with these tools. Because each Thinking Map represented a thinking *process* (cause and effect, sequencing, or categorizing), by using them, Michael was prompting his colleagues to both understand new content and actively interact with new ideas (see figures 3.1, 3.2, and 3.3, pages 42–44).

In figure 3.2, Michael used a Multi-Flow Map to guide participants in identifying elements that make a leadership team meeting successful. They used the same map to articulate the effects—or outcomes—they hoped would be a result of having had a successful meeting. In this process, participants in the meeting were able to establish criteria for their success (effects and outcomes) and explicitly state what they felt was needed to achieve these results (causes). By representing the thinking in a visual form, Michael was not only successful in capturing the attention of the other school leaders but also in engaging their thinking in a deep way. The visual representation supported the participants in identifying patterns in their responses as well as recognizing where important ideas might be missing. By co-constructing this map and the others, participants in the meeting were engaged in a highly focused and collaborative process with attention firmly rooted in the topics being discussed.

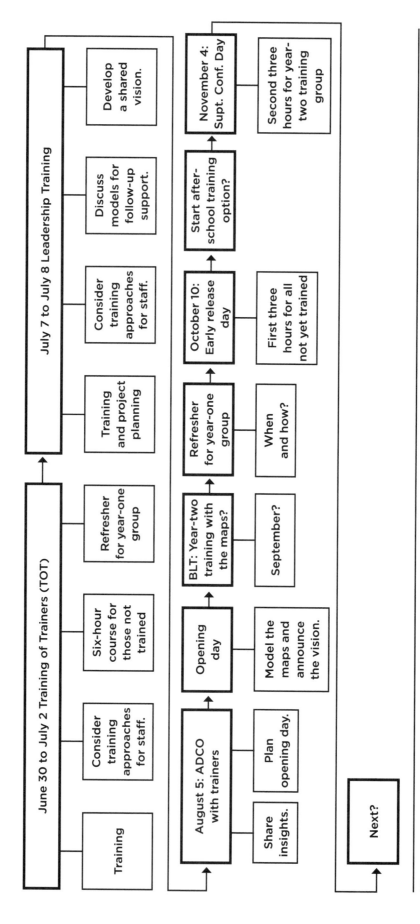

Figure 3.1: Sample Flow Map for Thinking Maps training.

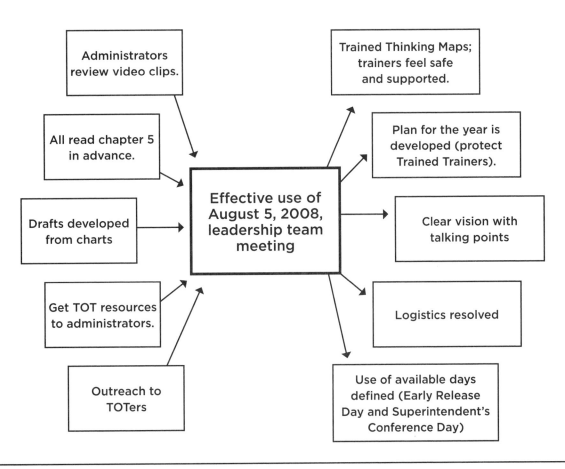

Figure 3.2: Sample Multi-Flow Map for leadership team meeting.

Michael knew this work well, believed in it, and was respected for his engagement in the implementation process. Others definitely viewed him as someone who walked the talk. Even so, Michael did not foresee the degree to which the ensuing events would challenge his belief in these tools and, consequently, his own reputation as a district leader.

Because of the delicacy of the situation and his reluctance to introduce something into the dynamic that might be perceived in the wrong way, Michael Sampson did not initially decide to use Thinking Maps to facilitate a resolution in this circumstance. However, the chair of the grievance committee and seventh-grade English teacher, Sharon Henderson, did. Sharon suggested to Michael that they use Thinking Maps to facilitate their meeting with the teacher, two principals, a union representative, and the grievance chair. Sharon described her decision to propose the use of Thinking Maps in this grievance situation.

> *The typical interaction was him [the principal] talking at her [the teacher] and her closing down and walking away. I was complaining [to Michael] about the principal's administrative style, and he defended the administrator—we had to find a way for it to work. I was using maps in my classroom, and I realized that when using the maps, I am not standing up here spouting*

Sedgwick Central School District: Thinking Maps Implementation

Cohort #1: 2007-2008	TOTers: Summer 2008	Leadership Team:	Cohort #2: Everyone Else 2008-2009	Building Leadership Teams	Parents	Students	Summer 2009 Follow-Up
Refresher: Fall 2008	Part of implementation team	Trained in summer 2008	Two three-hour sessions: October 10 and November 4	September and October	Orient to Thinking Maps initiative and facilitate their support for students	Step-up club?	BLTs?
Rubric: Self-assessment 2008	Orientation	Project plan for 2008-2009	TOTers? Additional integration support	Leadership training	Open house?	Student to student	Curriculum alignment teams
Goal setting: Moving to fluency with students	Cohort #2 Trainers	Collaboration with TOTers	Rubric: Self-assessment	Building leadership team plans	Parent evenings with kids?	Student to parents	Writing with Thinking Maps training
Introduce and discuss chapters 5 and 6.	Follow-up TOT support October 20-21	Ongoing support from Larry Alper	See Cohort #1.	Results and benchmarks		Student with teacher	Facilitate curriculum integration and differentiation project teams using Thinking Maps.
Curriculum integration with Thinking Maps	More training for Cohort #1?						
Writing with Thinking Maps: Write from the beginning, write for the future	Follow-up TOT support February 24						

Figure 3.3: Sample Tree Map for Thinking Maps implementation.

great knowledge—the maps are taking focus off me and putting the focus more on the students' thinking and the tool—the tool is speaking to kids, not me—the tool is generating thinking, not me—takes the focus off me as the expert and allows us all to work together as a team. . . . I had this realization that this was what was needed in this grievance situation. We needed to get visual focus off of us as individuals and onto a neutral focus both people focusing on the same thing—both looking down on this tool—use the tool to solve this problem.

Sharon astutely made the cognitive leap from the classroom to grievance setting. Just as the maps mediated the interaction between teachers, students, and ideas and experiences, Sharon saw the same possibility in a situation in which the constraints of role and emotions prevented communication at the level necessary to resolve this issue. Through the use of this common language, Sharon understood the important role the maps could play in shifting the focus from the people to the behaviors or teaching practices. Attention could jointly be directed to the aspects of the situation that needed to be addressed and to finding solutions, rather than to locating blame or defending positions. The externalization of the problem through the use of the maps provided a safe and constructive visual context for all involved to locate their attention. As Sharon notes, the maps create a collaborative space for people to construct ideas together and jointly pursue understanding. They focus on the content of the conflict and the ways to solve it, not on the people involved.

Changing Power Dynamics and Empowering Others

The hierarchical structure of schools and the way roles of authority are traditionally defined and exercised often impede the development of truly collaborative environments. Networking of ideas and interaction among members of the school community can't develop when lines of communication are rigidly defined and processes are not reciprocal. This constricted flow of thinking often leads predictably in a particular direction rather than toward the full expression of all the possibilities. Such cultures can certainly change, but doing so requires re-evaluating beliefs and then introducing new practices and reforming structures to align with the desired change in culture. The development of respectful and sustained conversations in building "equitable partnerships must be accompanied by district and school structures that replace hierarchy with networks and redefine roles, practices, and policies that have historically created and protected uneven power relationships" (Lambert et al., 1995, p. 100).

The use of Thinking Maps in group and interpersonal settings is inevitably collaborative. It begins with simple body language. When leaders begin to map out issues and identify steps to resolve them, they sit down side by side with a teacher or others with whom they are engaged in the mapping process. The physical orientation of the participants—focused together on the visual landscape of ideas they are co-creating—signals a power-sharing relationship.

The use of the maps also helps make thinking explicit. In interactions in which participants do not visually represent their ideas or do so in a narrow linear manner, statements may easily go unquestioned or carry weight without further examination. The cognitive patterns used to represent ideas in Thinking Maps, however, invite a level of questioning and precision that helps communication become clear and accountable. This can be critical to the outcome, particularly when emotions run high and the relationship of those involved is perceived as unequal.

Here's how Sharon Henderson, the grievance chairperson, described the impact of Thinking Maps in this situation:

> The teachers' union felt the principal was not being event specific [with the teacher]—the principal was using terms like always and never without specifics, and the teacher was like, "Prove it." The Thinking Map forced both parties to look at a particular incident and not do rabbit trailing—going to change the confrontation and the focal point. . . . It also gave the teacher something to walk away with that included her input. One thing that was important was that the administrator was not always holding the pencil—that she [the teacher] also got to hold the pencil and fill it [the Thinking Map] in. We have a very controlling administrator—tends to enjoy that controlling element. The use of the maps releases some of the administrative control and allows the teacher to take ownership.

This strategy has a couple advantages. First, the leader and the person being led share the responsibility to identify the problem and come up with a solution. Second, the maps allow both parties to focus more on the issues and less on the emotions. All leaders we interviewed agreed that sitting down with the maps diminished the emotional nature of these difficult situations with challenging teachers—even when the outcome was a firing.

As the meeting approached with his two building principals, the teacher, the grievance chair, and the head of the union, Michael remarked, "I had a sleepless night the night before thinking that if the Thinking Maps didn't work in this meeting they'd be dead at Sedgwick"— no one would want to use them again. He went on to say that his credibility as a leader was also at stake. He had invested much of his leadership career in this work and had professed his belief in these tools for student and adult learning and development. He had modeled the use of the maps in a variety of situations, demonstrated his knowledge and facility with them, and was being asked to apply this to a very real and intensely difficult situation.

In the case of the teacher with the grievance, she was retained, and the teacher improvement plan was dropped. Michael's successful application of the maps in this interaction affirmed his belief in these tools and, more importantly, allowed him to be faithful to his beliefs about communication and problem solving in school settings. As a leader, Michael is genuinely collaborative and holds an abiding faith in the ability of people to accomplish extraordinary things, even in the most challenging circumstances. Using the maps supported Michael in going forward in this interaction with an uncertain outcome, but he had confidence that clarity and constructive resolution could be achieved with everyone's dignity preserved or, in this case, restored.

Upon reflection, Sharon observed:

> There was a benefit that I never foresaw—not only did we use the maps to diffuse a problem and they were effective and I think will continue to be effective in event-specific issues . . . but what I never foresaw was the benefit from the improvement in the relationship between these two people [the principal and the grieving teacher]. For the first time ever, after the meeting, the teacher actually asked for input from the principal—she said it went quite well—this is a complete turn-around. . . . We'll have to see if it continues, but so far, so good. . . . I credit the maps with diffusing the problem and giving us a plan and a hope for the future.

Not only did the use of the maps help identify strategies for the teacher to improve and a way of resolving the conflict driving the grievance, but in the end, the use of the maps gave the two parties involved in this substantial conflict a language for talking with each other in the future. The teacher—who prior to the use of Thinking Maps refused to have any more conversations with the principal—now asked to work side by side with the principal to improve her classroom performance.

Experiences like this one have a way of empowering people directly and indirectly associated with the event. The successful outcome achieved through Sharon's and Michael's intervention and decision to use Thinking Maps to resolve a complex situation had ripple effects for them and their colleagues. Not surprisingly, their success in this situation encouraged them and others in the system to deepen and expand their use of this powerful language.

Michael discussed using the maps with his teachers when engaging in observations. Note the following example.

> With the amount of experience I've had with the maps and my background in cognitive coaching, I find this is an enormous asset to guide collaborative planning and also do coaching to guide reflection of particular individuals along the way. For example, one of my Thinking Maps trainers is doing a lesson tomorrow and sat down with me to do a preobservation conference—I'm going to be the observer. She used the Circle, Frame, and Tree Maps to outline the lesson for me. As we talked about what she wanted me to observe

in the lesson, together we constructed a Multi-Flow Map of the assessment/ evidence that would be available of what objectives to look for. We used another map together to plan for that observational assessment. It is in part my own evolution of knowing these Thinking Maps but also the fact that I'm willing to use them and allow teachers to see how much I value them.

As Michael observed, his ongoing use of the maps contributed to the development of his fluency with these tools. At the same time, his total engagement with them reinforces their use for teachers as well as models his own willingness to take risks and grow in his practice.

Sharon, the grievance chair, discussed how after this experience she started using the maps when teachers came to her with a grievance (figure 3.4). First, they would brainstorm all the issues using a Circle Map. Then, because these interactions are so emotionally laden, she would have the person potentially filing the grievance use a Bubble Map to describe all the emotions he or she felt about the event, issue, or experience.

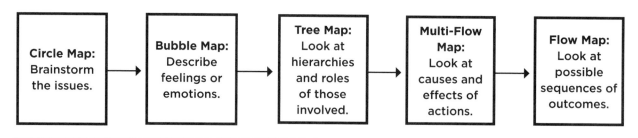

Figure 3.4: Sample Flow Map for grievance.

Sharon observed that it was very important to "validate emotions but then move on." The use of other Thinking Maps allowed the person involved to look more closely at the issue, develop a deeper understanding of it, and consider a range of possibilities before choosing a particular path. These experiences are intensely emotional, but by keeping attention on the maps—on the *thinking*—the issues remained in focus, meetings were productive, and tension and negative emotions were minimized.

Seeing Clearly

All the leaders using Thinking Maps in challenging interactions with teachers said the same thing—the maps increased clarity. In these instances, however, clarity was not to be confused with affirmation of a pre-existing belief or view of the situation. The clarity each leader achieved was associated with a change in his or her understanding of the problem through the visual rendition of the ideas. This visual processing of experience and thought—the outward projection of the inner workings of each leader's mind—was very much an *artistic* process, in the sense that the result, as Maxine Greene (1995) says, "is the possibility of looking at things as if they could be otherwise" (p. 16).

Each person's mind has its own internal topography through which new experiences and ideas travel. Its complex terrain develops over time through the forces of our accumulated experiences. We become rooted in the formations and resistant to alterations in the landscape. The more challenging a new situation is, the more complex and ambiguous it seems to be, and the more likely we are to revert to the internal constraints and structures that already exist and to which we are well acclimated.

However, in the type of situations leaders experience—high stakes, often of extreme emotional content—the ability to move beyond the conventions of one's thinking is essential to seeing the situation clearly and making genuinely informed decisions about what to do. The clarity these leaders struggled to attain would allow them to achieve a result clearly aligned with their personal beliefs, with the goals of the school, and with respect for all involved. The act of literally drawing out their thinking provided them with a method of raising to the surface their unconscious thoughts and feelings.

For these leaders, as we will see in the next case study, mapping out their thinking resembles the artistic act of drawing noted in chapter 1, as the artist Milton Glaser (2008) describes:

> What is most compelling to me about the act of drawing is that you become aware, or conscious of, what you are looking at only through the mechanism of trying to draw it. When I look at something I do not see it unless I make an internal decision to draw it. Drawing it in a state of humility provides a way for the truth to emerge. (p. 11)

Using Thinking Maps to visually manifest their ideas allowed these leaders to attend to complex circumstances in a highly attuned manner and see things with a heightened degree of clarity.

Acting Purposefully

Judy Kantor, an elementary principal in New York, described a difficult process with a nontenured teacher who, though bright and highly qualified, struggled to succeed with her students.

> Every district in New York does an APPR [Annual Personnel Performance Review] for teachers. We had to sit down in the early 1990s and come up with a plan on how one would evaluate teachers, including the union and administration. It became known as the APPR, and regardless of the district and slight variations on the theme, it is used collectively throughout the state. There are seven or eight headings using unsatisfactory to basic, proficient to superstar. Within that there is a rubric.
>
> I have a teacher—hired a year ago—who could teach and looked like she had a great rapport with children. Immediately, I noticed some issues stood out

as an ouch or an eww when I observed her—"something is not right here, but I can't put my finger on it." This woman is bright and should be successful, but I was constantly running interference with parents. Collectively, we would decide something she needed to work on, and it wouldn't get done—there was some component I couldn't put my finger on. Previously, we would've said she should be tenured.

An *ouch* and an *eww*—not a very solid foundation on which to design an intervention or provide helpful feedback to the individual to inform her practice. Judy's observation not only signaled areas that needed to be addressed but also indicated the discomfort she experienced in her observation—an emotional reaction that could easily trigger an emotional response. Aware of this, Judy turned to Thinking Maps to assist her in clearly articulating her thoughts before meeting with the teacher. She went on to describe the next steps in this process.

I created a Tree Map out of these rubrics and started writing down the observable behaviors and color-coded it—doing or not doing. The behaviors that clustered in certain areas of not doing came down to the affective domain. When I met with the teacher, I would target those issues I could help her with, and she could go to facilitators and work on the others—[such as] not following the curriculum map in her grade level, [or] parents saying homework was not making any sense.

Judy's use of the maps allowed her to achieve a level of clarity and focus so that she could engage the teacher in a productive interaction about her practice. From this conversation, she developed a plan of action, arranged support, and scheduled follow-up conferences.

By the end of the year, I was still dealing with these issues. Thinking Maps helped me because I could be very concrete about what we were talking about—the areas that needed to improve. For six weeks she was perfect, but then she just stopped doing what she agreed to improve upon. The union president spoke to her and told her that she was going to be fired. She could not seem to improve long term. I was able to be more matter of fact—focusing on the issues. The Thinking Maps made things very clear in my mind and allowed me to articulate it very well—hone in very specifically. It was still emotional for her loss of job, but I was very clear this is what we're talking about. Without the maps, I couldn't have been this clear—what's the problem, what are the strengths, and what do we need to work on. It really helped me as an administrator.

Judy's staff and peers acknowledge her as an outstanding school leader. She has extensive experience with supervising inexperienced teachers. She had documents and rubrics of what should be acceptable for a teacher and to assess teacher competency in the classroom, yet she still struggled to precisely identify the issues for this particular new teacher. However, as Judy acknowledged, the form of this information and the emotional complexity and implications of the interactions with this teacher—potential job loss, resistance, or inability to change—made it especially challenging to see the elements clearly.

Initially, Judy used the maps to unlock the constraints, internal and external, on her thought processes. Visually reformulating her ideas allowed her to see them in the context of this interaction and not simply as a reflection of past experiences. Although her ideas remained informed by her knowledge and professional history, she developed them directly in response to the particulars of this new situation. Glaser (2008) similarly describes his drawing of a portrait of his mother: "I could not see her as she existed in that moment until I became attentive by deciding to draw her. What I held in my mind was an accumulation of all my historical encounters with her" (p. 17). Preconceived ideas have the potential to inform or inhibit our thinking. For Judy, like Glaser, drawing out her ideas in response to the immediate circumstances of this experience enabled her to see them with greater clarity and a sure sense of purpose.

Once they sat down together with the documents—the observations and the Thinking Maps—Judy and the teacher could identify the issues. In this situation, the teacher had been unable to sustain any improvement she made based on Judy's feedback and support. However, as Judy pointed out later in her interview, the maps made it possible to clearly articulate what had been agreed on and where progress was still lacking. Although this process resulted in the nonrenewal of the teacher's contract, using Thinking Maps made this challenging experience much more focused and evidence based. A significant reason for this, as in the previous example, was that the negative emotions and acrimony typically associated with such interactions were greatly reduced. The visual representation of the record and analysis of the classroom observations enabled the dialogue to remain focused on the teacher's practice and the results or lack thereof.

Emotions play an important role in bringing our attention to critical aspects of a situation. We need to recognize and respond to these signals. However, because of our accumulated experiences and histories and the uncertainty that accompanies these moments of heightened intensity, there is always the risk that our vision will be blurred and our responses to events will be confused. As another leader in Judy's school observed, "Meetings that rely primarily on verbal exchanges often leave ideas and emotions hanging unresolved."

Judy's use of Thinking Maps created an opportunity to become clear about her thoughts, perceptions, and purpose. In use with the teacher, the maps enabled the focus of the interaction to remain on the teacher's practice, not the person. This minimized the power dynamics as the maps provided an emergent landscape to display, consider, and support ideas with evidence. The actions taken throughout this process were not based on opinions or preconceived ideas of what should be done, but directly related to the content generated through the ensuing dialogues and co-construction of the maps.

Minimizing the discomfort and anxiety these situations can induce is a significant factor in thinking clearly, expansively, and compassionately. The intricacies and delicacy of human dynamics in the workplace require skillful and thoughtful responses. Issues of moral and ethical complexity are commonplace in school settings as critical decisions are constantly being made under challenging circumstances such as limited resources, lack of time, and general uncertainty regarding the outcomes.

As a brain-compatible tool, Thinking Maps reduce anxiety by providing familiar patterns for thinking and working with complex ideas, situations, and emotions. The metacognitive awareness that the maps promote allows emotions to inform thinking without distorting the process. For school leaders, this is a particularly important trait to develop as their actions, by the very nature of their role relationship with those around them, are as symbolic as they are real and reverberate throughout the school community. We are reminded, again, of Daniel Goleman's observation, "The continual interplay of limbic open loop systems among members in a group creates a kind of emotional soup, with everyone adding his or her own flavors to the mix. *But it is the leader who adds the strongest seasoning* [italics added]" (Goleman, Boyatzis, & McKee, 2002, p. 8).

The use of Thinking Maps in the highly charged situations we described in this chapter enabled both Michael and Judy to slow the process down—first for themselves and then for those with whom they interacted. In doing so, they gave themselves an opportunity to develop clarity, both in purpose and in understanding the nature of the challenge. Having the support of these tools reassured them that the ambiguity and complexity of the circumstances were not beyond their ability to work with and grasp.

In the next chapter, we will investigate how the use of Thinking Maps in the context of supervising, evaluating, coaching, and mentoring enabled such interactions to remain focused on growth and learning in the practice of teaching despite the anxiety and stress often associated with these processes. In these accounts, the themes of empowerment along with personal clarity emerge.

Interpersonal Thinking

The two examples in chapter 3 focused on extreme but not unfamiliar situations in schools, situations in which all the complexity of human relationships comes into play. In the final section of this chapter, we will turn our attention to teachers' experiences in regular coaching and supervision settings; that is, those settings in which leaders use Thinking Maps to promote growth and development rather than to resolve crises. To what degree, if any, is the experience for teachers whose employment may not be in question, but whose practice is being closely scrutinized, made different through the use of Thinking Maps?

Enhancing Teacher Effectiveness

In her work on promoting growth and excellence in teachers, Charlotte Danielson (1996) observes, "Through reflection, real growth and therefore excellence are possible. By trying to understand the consequences of actions and by contemplating alternative courses of action, teachers expand their repertoire of practice" (p. 106). Many years before Danielson made this statement, John Dewey (1998) proposed that we learn not from experience but from reflecting on it. Both views identify the ability to reflect as a core disposition necessary for achieving and sustaining excellence in one's practice.

Donald Schön (1987) describes this level of practice as *professional artistry*, in which the ability to reflect in action is crucial to the development of professional competence. As Schön writes, "This kind of reflection-in-action is central to the artistry with which practitioners sometimes make new sense of uncertain, unique, or conflicted situations" (p. 35). Teaching is full of daily interactions with learners that require more than a formulaic response or standard intervention; teachers are required to draw on their knowledge and experience to respond to individual needs and strengths appropriately. Professional artistry in teaching requires the practitioner to respond confidently in the face of ambiguity and, if necessary, reframe the problem or challenge in light of current realities. Such adeptness allows teachers to take into account conventional rules, assumptions, and existing models with the agility and confidence to go beyond them.

Ambiguity can be seen as either an obstacle or an opportunity. In response to what Schön (1987, p. 6) describes as the often "indeterminate zones of practice," reflective practitioners do what is required of all successful people when faced with uncertainty—they *think*.

Art Costa (2008b) points out that while the ability to think is innate and spontaneous—we are wired to think, at the very least, to survive—"skillful thinking must be cultivated" (p. 20). Coaching reflective practice, therefore, is less about correcting practice than about developing teachers' ability to mediate their own learning. The leader in this role has much the same goal as a teacher. Both want their students not only to develop an understanding of the content but also to become aware of their thinking processes. In this way, the adult learners—the teachers—like their students, are not bound by their experiences but use each one to refine and, more importantly, improve their ability to think about their practice. The confidence that comes from reflecting on and evaluating their decisions increases the likelihood that teachers will fluidly and skillfully consider and select approaches that respond to the needs of a given situation rather than rely on formulaic, predetermined models. At their highest level of artistry, reflective teachers do this as their interactions with students unfold, in addition to doing so afterward.

In the following two case studies, we examine how the use of Thinking Maps in the coaching and supervision context enabled school leaders to fulfill their intended goals of developing skillful thinking for newly hired teachers and those with extensive experience in the profession. The case studies also present the interactions from the teachers' points of view. What about the use of Thinking Maps made these experiences different from the traditional approaches in which they had previously participated?

Developing Skillful Thinking

In 2007, St. Robert of Newminster Catholic School and Sixth Form College in England introduced Thinking Maps to all staff as a key strategy to support the development of thinking. It was believed that teachers' use of Thinking Maps would help shift the focus of the educational experience to students, that teachers' collaboration and conversation would become more focused, and that these new dispositions and skills would lead to greater coherence in their beliefs and practices about teaching *for* learning. The effectiveness of the teaching, too, was expected to be significantly enhanced for all members of the school community. A complete description of St. Robert's own research on Thinking Maps is available from the Thinking Foundation (n.d.c) website (www.thinkingfoundation.org).

As the implementation got underway at St. Robert, the staff—teachers and administrators—recognized a unique opportunity to integrate the use of Thinking Maps into teacher professional development. This, they believed, would be congruent with their efforts to highlight and elevate thinking as the central goal of their instructional program. They hypothesized that applying Thinking Maps in this way with the faculty would lead to increased effectiveness in their instructional abilities and a rise in student achievement. "We hope to prove," the St. Robert researchers write, "that as a consequence of a deliberate immersion strategy of adopting a *cognitive approach* [italics added] to Teacher Professional Development—i.e. Thinking Maps in training, teacher observation and feedback, mentoring and coaching—teacher confidence and effectiveness will increase" (Thinking Foundation, n.d.c, p. 5).

St. Robert had followed traditional methods for providing feedback and setting goals for improvement for Newly Qualified Teachers (NQTs). Here the school describes its typical process.

This usually involved the observer reading from his or her linear notes,
attempting to focus in on aspects of the lesson that went well in order to
encourage the NQT to continue adopting specific strategies that worked,
and identifying elements of planning and delivery that did not work so well
in order to generate possible strategies for improving teacher performance.
(Thinking Foundation, n.d.c, p. 16)

The leaders at St. Robert, having begun the implementation of Thinking Maps and acutely focused on cognitive development, noticed a distinct misalignment between their existing coaching practices and their desire to promote the NQTs' reflective thinking. A major constraint inherent in the current process was the teachers' lack of access to the observers' notes. It was difficult to determine if the observers' recall of the events represented the session accurately or selectively. Additionally, because the observers controlled the information and often sat across from the teacher, they immediately reinforced power dynamics, making it difficult for the NQTs to remain objective about the lesson during the feedback. As the St. Robert researchers note, the NQTs often found themselves "regarding comments intended to improve classroom performance in a negative manner," reducing their self-esteem, inhibiting their thinking, and creating a barrier for growth through the existing process (Thinking Foundation, n.d.c, p. 16). The research team developed a Bubble Map (figure 4.1, page 56) to describe the qualities of the traditional feedback method used before the introduction of Thinking Maps into the process.

Each descriptor in the Bubble Map represents a quality of the interaction that would significantly interfere with the thinking processes of each NQT involved. Wanting to move beyond the show-and-tell approach to classroom observation and feedback—the teachers show, and the observers tell and interpret what they see—the school leaders at St. Robert introduced Thinking Maps into the coaching process. They hoped to create an interactive setting where the NQTs could more easily identify and understand the elements of teaching and learning that were in need of improvement. The partial Multi-Flow Map (figure 4.2, page 57) represents how they believed the use of Thinking Maps would support this type of interaction.

The use of Thinking Maps represents a fundamental shift in the power dynamics of the interaction, with transparency now a central feature of the experience. Thinking Maps promoted a collaborative process in which the NQT mediated his or her own learning and made decisions for how to improve with the support of the coach.

Lesson debriefs began with an NQT being given the opportunity to describe the lesson. This process allowed time for the NQT to reflect on the experience. The description set the agenda for the ensuing discussion. Beginning in this way allowed the NQT's experience to become the central feature of the interaction. While the coach would observe this particular lesson,

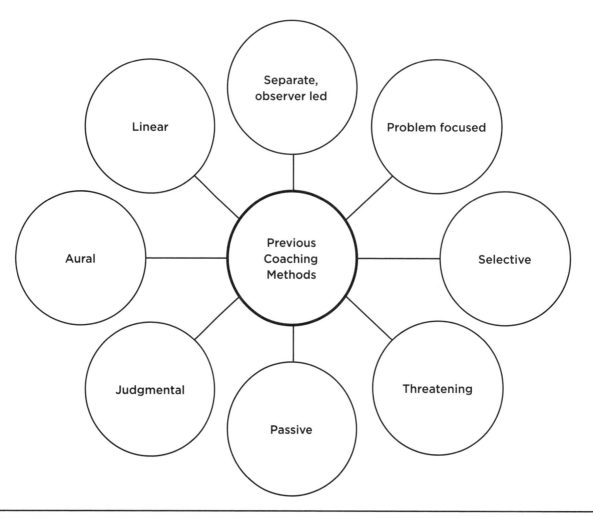

Figure 4.1: Sample Bubble Map of the traditional feedback method.

the teacher would be alone with his or her experience for the overwhelming majority of the school year. The coach immediately signaled to the NQT that the goal of this interaction was to support the teacher in developing his or her ability to reflect on and learn from his or her experience in the classroom. The use of Thinking Maps provided the NQT with a tool for externalizing the experience, for seeing it in a way that allowed connections to be made and a critical analysis to form. For the NQT, as for the students in the class, Thinking Maps became tools for mediating one's own learning.

The observer (or coach) guided the NQT in the use of a series of Thinking Maps to then probe the experience, articulate and identify key elements in the teaching practices and decisions, and promote a dialogue of inquiry about the NQT's pedagogy. The Bubble Map provided the observer with an opportunity to help the NQT surface his or her feelings about the lesson and the reasons behind them. Next, the NQT used a Double Bubble Map to compare and contrast impressions of the lesson with the Bubble Map from a previous observation (figure 4.3, page 58). The areas in contrast allowed the teacher to identify and discuss the planned changes he or she made prior to conducting the new lesson in order to

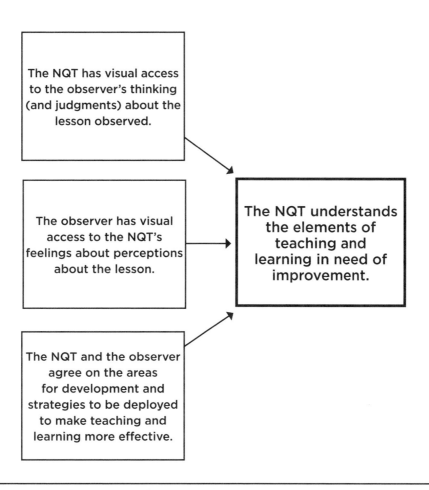

Figure 4.2: Sample partial Multi-Flow Map for NQT training.

seek improvement. Each step reinforced the teacher's thinking by visually representing his or her thought processes as well as the content of the experience.

The observer also used Thinking Maps to communicate information. The observer created a Flow Map during the observation of the lesson, which made the structure of the lesson, key events, planned tasks, and transitions between teacher and learner activity visible to the NQT. This visual storytelling also provided the NQT with an opportunity to go back into the experience and add to the narrative. Together, the NQT and the observer reconstructed the story of the lesson and continued the process of collaborative inquiry into the experience. An NQT commented on this benefit, "It is a lot easier to view the lesson if it is presented sequentially. I was surprised how logical it is and it is easier for both of you to see it and discuss it" (Thinking Foundation, n.d.c, p. 21). The focus on the Flow Map allowed for easy movement into an effective discussion about aspects of planning, teacher behavior, learner behavior, and outcomes.

Following the lesson debrief, the observer and the NQT summarized the teacher's performance using Tree Maps (see figures 4.4 and 4.5, pages 59–60).

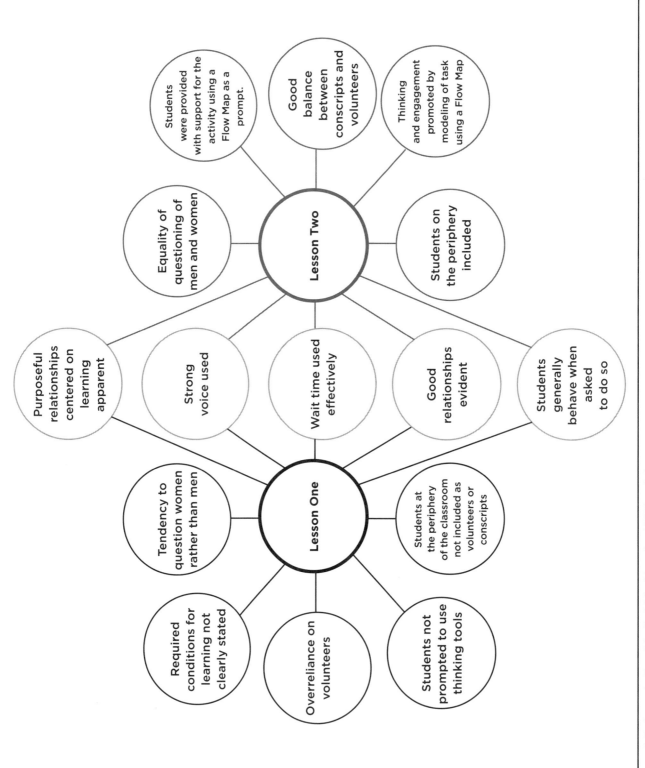

Figure 4.3: Sample Double Bubble Map for NQT training.

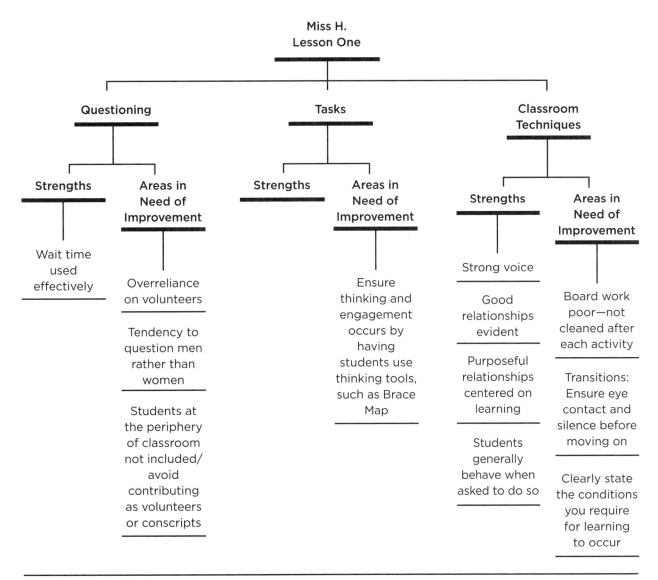

Figure 4.4: Sample Tree Map to summarize teacher performance in lesson one.

They reported that the use of the Tree Maps allowed for the target setting to become more focused on the discrete aspects of teaching and learning. The visual representation clearly highlighted those pedagogical processes that were effectively employed and those aspects that needed to be changed for increased effectiveness. Here again, the use of Thinking Maps ensured that the discussion regarding next steps would remain focused and precise.

As a result of using Thinking Maps, in one particular interaction between an observer and an NQT, the researchers at St. Robert reported that the ensuing discussions promoted:

- Clarification and negotiation about the validity of statements that each party made

- An opportunity for the NQT to generate his or her own ideas about how the lesson could have been improved

- A valuable discussion about the potential strategies the observer could offer the NQT in the future

- A discussion about shifts in planning that may need to occur to enhance effectiveness of similar lessons in the future

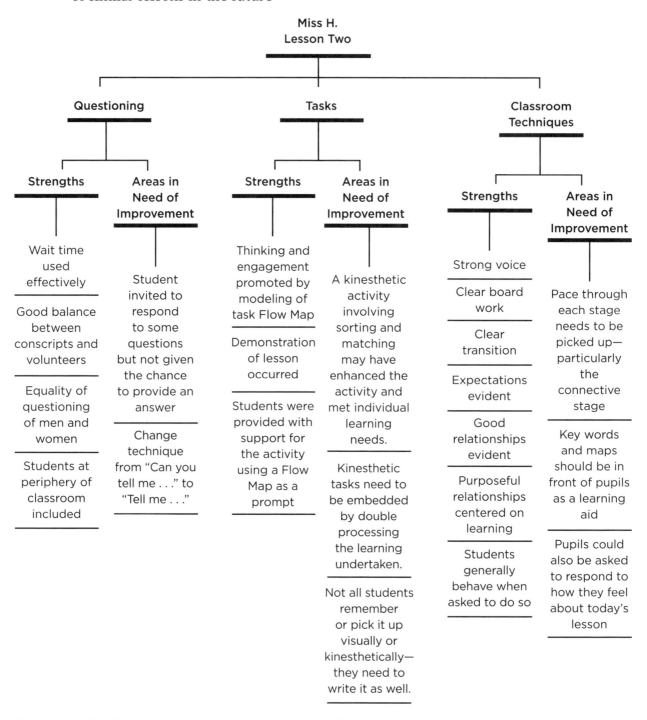

Figure 4.5: Sample Tree Map to summarize teacher performance in lesson two.

They reported that the added value of using Thinking Maps was that offering the NQT access to a visual map of the lesson meant that the map itself, or the NQT's teaching practice—not the teacher—became the object of discussion about performance. One NQT commented, "There was a lot less pressure. We could focus on things that make an effective lesson and for me to concentrate on. The maps can also be kept as a form of reference in my file for me to refer back to" (Thinking Foundation, n.d.c, p. 21).

As her comments suggest, each Thinking Map became an instrument of learning, a dynamic space for shared concern and interest, forming the basis for a dignified exchange of ideas and a collaborative inquiry process. The maps formed the third corner of the triangle connecting the newly qualified teacher and supervisor to the teaching experience that had been observed, allowing the observer and the NQT to join together in a common pursuit of learning. The map of the teaching event, not the teacher herself, became the object of discussion. The map "allowed the fostering of a relationship based upon mutual respect for each other's roles," the researchers at St. Robert reported. "The NQT moved from being merely a recipient of negative feedback towards being an active partner in a co-constructive relationship" (Thinking Foundation, n.d.c, p. 18). This was made evident in the Bubble Map the NQT used to reflect on this aspect of the experience with Thinking Maps (figure 4.6).

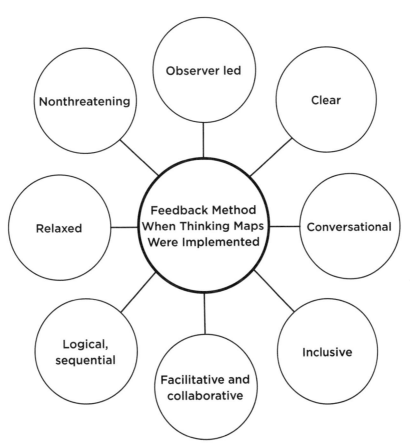

Figure 4.6: Sample Bubble Map of the NQT's experience using Thinking Maps.

Consistent with the NQT's goals for his or her students, the use of Thinking Maps in the coaching process promoted and supported the NQT's ability to grow in autonomy to mediate his or her own learning.

The research from St. Robert clearly points to the success of using Thinking Maps in the coaching process with teachers early in their development. In this last section, we will look at what our research revealed about the impact of this approach when used with highly skilled and experienced practitioners.

Coaching Professional Artistry

The complex nature of teaching requires people who can respond to multiple demands and recognize opportunities—teachable moments—in dynamic and often challenging environments. Successful teachers are frequently described as thoughtful, self-aware practitioners with the facility to adjust their actions in the moment as well as to reflect afterward. Such *professional artistry* (Schön, 1987) is demonstrated by the teacher's ability to continually assess the results of his or her decisions through the responses of his or her students and to create new approaches as needed. While the coaching of beginning teachers addresses their cognitive development, it also focuses extensively on building pedagogical skills and resources. With experienced, highly qualified teachers, effective coaching and supervision needs to assist and support teachers in developing and refining their abilities to think analytically, abstractly, autonomously, and flexibly.

Kathy Ernst (in press), an experienced educator, coach, and author, worked closely with graduate students pursuing leadership roles in education. As part of her process of developing their skills as leaders, Kathy guided them through a coaching cycle quite different from those they had previously experienced. For the leaders in training to work at another level with those they, in turn, would coach and supervise, Kathy introduced them to the use of Thinking Maps as tools for facilitating professional learning and growth. She notes, "Skillfully used, Thinking Maps are powerful tools for building and sustaining a culture of collaboration, trust, inquiry, and learning in the coaching and supervision cycles" (Ernst, in press). Commenting on the effects of the use of the maps on the development of teachers' ability to think about and reflect on their practice, Kathy adds, "The maps mediate cognitive shifts by providing teachers with a visible lens through which the teacher can *see* and *understand* the need to change their practice" (Ernst, in press). Here again, as previously detailed in the experience at St. Robert, the use of Thinking Maps was seen as critical in the development of people's ability to think about and shape their own practice.

As Kathy began to examine her existing practice, she asked herself several key questions (Ernst, 2011, p. 179):

> *How could I more clearly and efficiently document events as I was observing and making notes in the classroom?*

How could I shift the locus of control from me to us in the post-conference by making the display and retrieval of observation data transparent and visible—and more inclusive and democratic for teachers?

How could my use of the lesson data facilitate a nonthreatening, collaborative inquiry and analysis focused on student learning and the teaching—not on the teacher?

Kathy's process of examining her supervision practice to align it with her outcomes for teachers mirrored the process she intended to use when guiding teachers in reflecting on their own work. She questioned whether her strategies were congruent with the thoughtful, reflective approach she wanted teachers to apply to their coaching and supervision practices. The use of Thinking Maps, she concluded, would enable her to be explicit, effective, and efficient in her interactions with teachers and promote an inquiry process essential to learning.

The following examples demonstrate how Kathy used Thinking Maps at various stages of the coaching and supervision cycle with teachers to make descriptive data visible and available for further analysis. She used a Flow Map (figure 4.7, page 64) to record the sequence of events during the lesson observation, and later, she and a teacher used it to reconstruct the event and add anything that might have been missed. This document of the lesson and the interaction Kathy and the teacher engaged in established a climate of transparency, equity, and trust.

The reading or retelling of the lesson story allowed the teacher to go back into the experience and surface key aspects of it that might otherwise have been lost to memory. From this process of retelling, the teacher and Kathy identified areas of focus for deeper analysis. Using Multi-Flow Maps (figure 4.8, page 65) gave the teacher an opportunity to examine causes and effects of various teaching moves and play out alternatives. The questions Kathy used and the Thinking Maps they created together enabled the teacher to *see* her practice, question it, propose alternatives to her decisions, and prepare for the next lesson with greater clarity and new insights.

The Tree Map used in postconference meetings (figure 4.9, page 66) provides teachers with a roadmap, articulating areas in the lesson that need improvement and identifying next instructional steps in response to student-specific actions. In this Tree Map of a different lesson, the teacher articulates the teaching moves she felt had advanced student learning and what she believed she needed to do to improve her effectiveness.

The final subcategory of the Tree Map gave the teacher and Kathy the opportunity to discuss and identify specific actions the teacher could take to make the necessary improvements in her practice. Kathy's skillful use of the Tree Map engaged the teacher in analyzing a specific teaching-learning interaction and challenged her to consider how the improvements in that lesson could be generalized in her teaching.

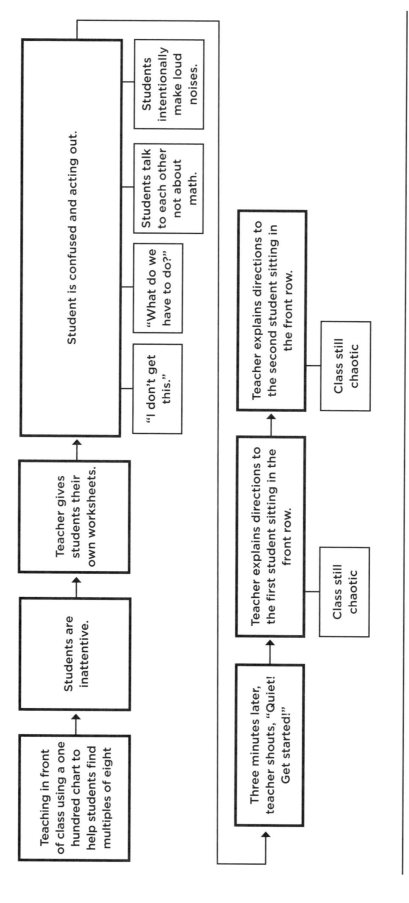

Figure 4.7: Sample Flow Map for math-lesson observation.

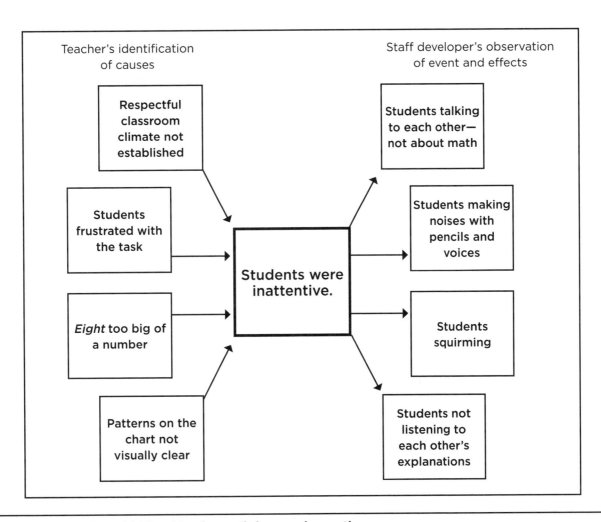

Figure 4.8: Sample Multi-Flow Map for math-lesson observation.

For Kathy, using Thinking Maps was a vehicle for promoting the reflective conversations she believed were necessary for teachers to construct the pedagogical content knowledge required for improving student learning: "Since reflective conversations are rooted in rich, descriptive, readily accessible observation data, opportunities for teachers to deepen their understanding of mathematics and children's development of mathematical ideas are maximized" (Ernst, in press).

However, what do the teachers think about this process? One teacher Kathy worked with described the impact on her ability to mediate her own learning in this way.

> Better than a film, the map both isolates each move that teacher and students make and shows those moves as they connect and lead to one another. When we reviewed the maps, I noticed patterns in the frequency of certain types of moves and also saw patterns within series of moves. As we looked at the series of moments, I considered what kinds of questions and prompts I used. Are they open enough? Do the students respond by

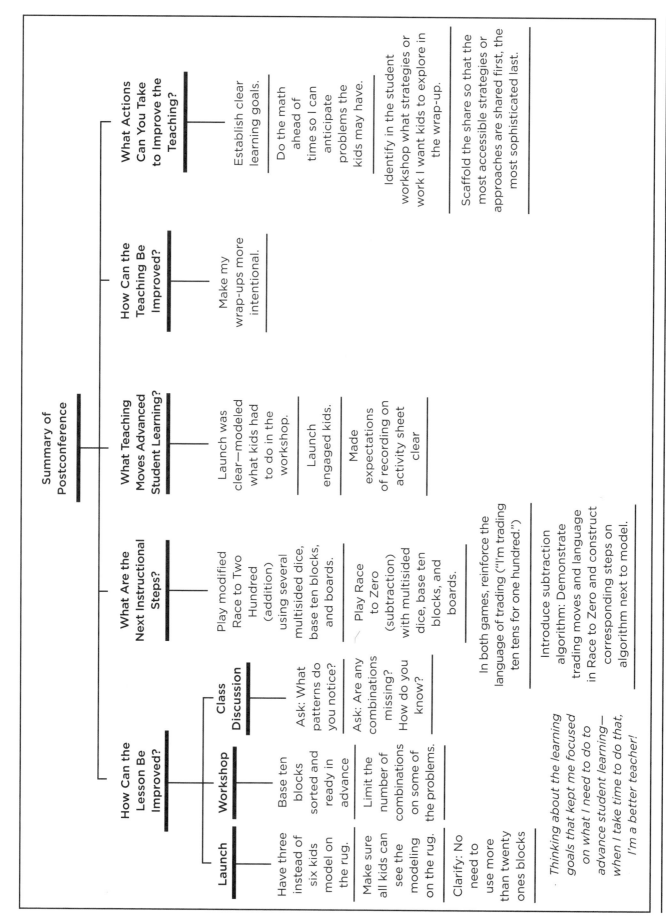

Figure 4.9: Sample Tree Map for math-lesson observation.

offering thoughtful answers that show understanding, or do they respond with short, simple answers? Do I accept short, simple answers, or do I probe for explanations and understanding? Do I accept the right answer too quickly, letting students off the hook without exploring their thinking and bringing the other students along? These kinds of questions are difficult to explore based on the memory of a lesson. However, when you look at the map and you can see the words that you chose, the reaction(s) you received, and where that series of actions led the class, you really can think about "What would have happened if I . . ." (K. Ernst, personal communication with M. Fitzgerald, February 17, 2007)

Notice the reflective questions the teacher asked herself in this process. Not only had the maps provided her with a detailed landscape of her work to examine but they gave her an opportunity to hone her ability to articulate questions that she could ask herself in future teaching-learning interactions, with or without the presence of the coach.

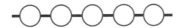

As we have seen from the case studies in this chapter, the nature of the interaction between people was key to the outcomes achieved. Relationships that were or became supported by trust, transparency, and reciprocity opened the space for learning and growth to occur. The reciprocal processes enhanced by the use of Thinking Maps in these relationships directly empowered the individuals involved to construct meaning and formulate new direction for their practice. Wheatley (1999) states, "If power is the capacity generated by our relationships, then we need to be attending to the *quality* of those relationships" (p. 40). As evidenced by the reflective comments of the leaders and teachers, the use of Thinking Maps broke down traditional barriers, fixed roles in the interactions, and allowed the participants to co-create ideas and discover for themselves the directions to take in their efforts to do more effective work. As Kathy Ernst reflected on her work, she recognized that her coaching and supervision practice needed to change in order to match the outcomes she hoped to achieve:

If the intent of the coaching/supervision experience is for teachers to reflect on my observations and integrate my notes with their own cognitive map of what happened and why during the lesson, it is incumbent upon me to offer the most visible record of my version of the classroom experience. (Ernst, in press)

The use of Thinking Maps allowed her to create a fundamental shift in the quality of her interactions so that the ability of teachers to *think* about their practice was the central focus of the coaching and supervision experience.

Entering into or committing to a reciprocal relationship means that "we give up predictability for potential" (Lambert, 1998, p. 36). Leaders as teachers recognize the value to the individual and the school in fostering such relationships. They understand that sustainable schools depend on the ability of everyone associated to be empowered as thinkers and decision makers. Schools are dynamic, complex places. They are constantly evolving and continually challenged by social, political, and economic realities. Sustainable schools require those within them to be fluid, agile thinkers capable of responding to emerging situations and open to the possibilities that such a dynamic state represents. The practices we use and the structures we put in place must support development of these individual and collective dispositions. As Daniel Goleman and colleagues (2002) suggest, "In the best processes, people have learned to learn. . . . They have a road map that makes sense to them" (p. 245). In these examples, our research shows how leaders and teachers used Thinking Maps as tools for meaningful engagement with each other. Their use of the maps deepened their ability to assume responsibility for their own growth and development. As Goleman et al. (2002) state, the benefit of becoming able to mediate one's own learning is "enhanced capacity to change" (p. 245), without which schools could not remain effective.

In the next chapter, we will examine how a new superintendent introduced the use of Thinking Maps into a district and transformed it into a learning community.

5

Collaborative Thinking

The schools in the Canisteo-Greenwood Central School District in which Jeff Matteson had just assumed the position of superintendent in 2008 had been identified as "in need of improvement" based on the previous year's scores on the New York State assessments. This came as a sharp rebuke to the district that had operated in a somewhat complacent manner in recent years. Serving over a thousand students from eleven townships in three comprehensive sites with two hundred employees, the district represented a range of stakeholders across the socioeconomic and political spectrum.

Jeff and his new administrative team reviewed the improvement plan that had been developed prior to his arrival. Together they determined that the plan lacked the reach necessary to move the district beyond a direct response to test scores. While the areas addressed in the plan were thought to be necessary, they were not well articulated. Nor were they developed with enough depth to ensure that the district's educational program would move beyond a quick fix to a more substantive educational transformation. An opportunity to do so would clearly be lost without a more comprehensive vision and concerted action on the part of the leadership team.

Of immediate concern, however, was how to spend $50,000 that needed to be allocated or it would be lost. Jeff convened a meeting of his team, knowing that if he simply asked them to identify how best to spend this money, each person would likely advocate for a particular project without taking into account the larger picture. He also knew that the meeting could quickly devolve into a competition for the money. Positional thinking would obscure the possibilities, and precious funds, along with an equally precious opportunity, could be lost. Having been trained in the use of Thinking Maps in a previous district, Jeff drew on them and designed the following process to achieve these tangible results:

- Before determining what to spend the money on, the administrative team used the Frame of Reference to identify the key forces that would and should influence its thinking. This allowed the group members to suspend judgment and together identify the forces in their individual and collective frame.

- The process of framing their thinking brought the group members together and enabled them to relax their individual impulses to determine the *what* before they fully appreciated the challenge and opportunity before them. As Michael Fullan (2003) says, "Premature clarity is a dangerous thing" (p. 29).

- The visual display of the thinking allowed ideas to emerge and connect in ways that would have been more difficult without the opportunity for group members to see each other's ideas. The school leaders were figuratively and, in the end, literally, on the same page. The maps provided a concrete, emergent representation of their individual and collective thinking and, in the process, connected them in the co-construction of meaning.

- Prioritizing the forces in the Frame promoted more discussion, deepened the appreciation for each person's ideas and contributions, and enlarged the field from which the group could go on to determine how best to apply these funds.

- The group used the Circle Map to identify possible ways to apply these funds; this reflected the collective thinking of the group and its shared goals for the system.

Working Toward a More Comprehensive and Shared Vision

At the start of this process, Jeff used a Circle Map to establish group norms (figure 5.1). On entering an already-established group, Jeff decided it was important for him and the administrators to articulate what they believed was necessary to function successfully as a leadership team.

This step proved wise and effective. Commenting on this particular aspect of the experience, one administrator observed, "Setting norms for our meetings was great because Jeff was the new person. . . . We were a little apprehensive. [The Circle Map] made it very easy to adjust to a new setting." The use of the visual shifted attention from the people involved to the needs of the group required for it to function effectively.

Through his use of Thinking Maps, Jeff began the process of establishing new cultural norms while at the same time addressing an immediate concern. He understood that, as Peter Senge states, "The way organizations are is a product of how we think and how we interact; they cannot change in any fundamental way unless we can change our basic patterns of thinking and interacting" (as cited in Galagan, 1991, p. 38). Therefore, if thinking became the foundation for the administrative team's interactive processes and, subsequently, for interactions throughout all aspects of the system, they would have to introduce new tools and collaborative patterns. As one member of the administrative team observed:

> *This was the first time we had gotten together as an administrative team. We didn't know what the maps were when Jeff pulled them out—we could have had that discussion around the table, but seeing it with the Frame of Reference, we all felt included. We felt like we had input and were listened to.*

Jeff's decision to use Thinking Maps successfully signaled and advanced an alternative to the impulse to achieve clarity and certainty prematurely. He also sent another essential message. As one senior administrator observed, "He walks the talk."

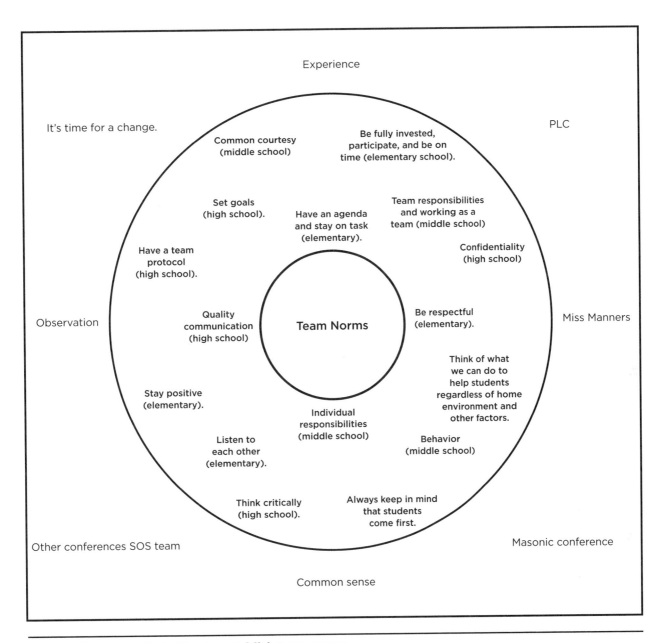

Figure 5.1: Sample Circle Map to establish team norms.

A core purpose in learning organizations is to move beyond the centrality of any one person's understanding of the topic or issue being addressed. What is essential, according to Senge (1990a), is "free exploration that brings to the surface the full depth of people's experience and thought and yet can move beyond their individual views" (p. 241). Jeff's skillful use of Thinking Maps to support an inquiry approach effectively and efficiently shifted the focus of the interaction from positions to possibilities. Using these tools and processes, members of the administrative team were able to suspend judgment and focus on the generation of ideas as opposed to the competition of interests.

As Jeff observed with evident satisfaction, the team accomplished the process in a manner that united its members around common principles and beliefs and reinforced their efficacy as leaders of a system, not just of individual schools.

They completed the process of ultimately deciding how to use the funds, which could otherwise have taken an excessive amount of time, in half an hour. More important than the efficient use of time, the decision itself resulted in a comprehensive professional development plan that addressed the deeper significance of the district's designation of "in need of improvement" and reflected and advanced its core values about teaching and learning. The transformation had begun.

A year later, Jeff and his administrative team achieved similar results as they skillfully and artfully used Thinking Maps to analyze data, develop an action plan, and subsequently guide the school board through a process of developing a vision for its system and identifying goals to achieve it. This time, however, all members of the leadership team were familiar and comfortable with the use of Thinking Maps. Applying multiple Thinking Maps (figure 5.2), the administrative team and the school board produced a five-year strategic plan (figure 5.3, page 74) on one piece of paper in three hours and twenty minutes. Jeff made special note of this last fact when describing the experience. However, more than the speed, the efficient and meaningful use of time and the total engagement of the board and the administrative team generated such enthusiasm from Jeff: "They never took a break, they were so into it—all were contributing, everything was positive and moving forward." Reflecting on the experience, he stated:

I'm really proud of this work. The board was open to the process and they were extremely productive. Imagine seven community members volunteering their Saturday in the summer to do this work! They will be adopting the plan at their next meeting. . . . Can't wait!

Leading Thinkers

In the months between these two experiences, Jeff led the implementation of Thinking Maps in his district. From the onset of his tenure as superintendent, Jeff established that he was indeed a leader who thought through the challenges he faced. As one of his colleagues observed, "He has a dream and follows through and is personally involved in the follow-through." In the ensuing months, he also demonstrated that he was equally committed to developing the capacity of everyone within the community of the school system to do the same. More than being a thinking leader, Jeff was leading thinkers throughout the system.

As part of the transformative process to create a thinking school system, Jeff identified a highly skilled and respected group of faculty members to train colleagues in the implementation of Thinking Maps. The teachers, in turn, introduced these tools to their students with the same goal in mind—to transfer the use of these cognitive navigational tools to the students

---

**Board of Education Vision and Goal-Setting
Workshop Planning Model
August 29, 2009**

1. **Flow Map:** Historical perspective
   Questions:
   - ○ Frame—Characterize the last five years of our school district's history (turning points, accomplishments, events, and so on).
   - ○ Complete the following sentence—"The year 2004 was the beginning of the age of _____."
   - ○ How would we want the school to be characterized three to five years from now? The age of _____? **Translate this into a guiding philosophy.**

2. **Tree Map:** Describe district strengths, weaknesses, opportunities, and threats (three each).

3. **Bubble Map:** Use adjectives to describe Canisteo-Greenwood graduates.

4. **Circle Map:** Describe the 21st century world in which our students will love, work, and contribute.

5. **Bubble Map:** Use adjectives to describe high school graduates with 21st century skills.

6. **Double Bubble Map:** Compare and contrast current Canisteo-Greenwood graduations and graduates with 21st century skills.

7. **Circle Map:** Describe a successful school. (Identify a phrase that describes our **vision** of a successful school.)

8. **Double Bubble Map:** Compare and contrast our school today with our vision.

9. **Circle Map:** Describe all the parts of this district's educational system to consider when setting district goals (break down to five).

10. **Tree Map:** Consider five parts of the educational system that are most likely to transform the vision into reality **(goals).**

Figure 5.2: Model of strategic plan using Thinking Maps.

for their skillful and independent use across all learning contexts, both in and beyond the school setting.

At the same time, Jeff arranged for his core leadership team to participate in the Thinking Maps leadership training. During the initial two days of this training, the members of the leadership team were introduced to the use of Thinking Maps for the full range of leadership practices, including analyzing data, coaching and supervision, facilitating meetings across a broad range of topics and contexts, establishing goals and visions, and doing program evaluation and development. Most significantly, however, these school leaders were provided the

Teaching for Learning
CANISTEO-GREENWOOD CENTRAL SCHOOL DISTRICT

STRATEGIC PLAN 2009–2014

Vision
Success for all students

Mission
Teaching for learning for all students at optimum levels

Core Values

Learning	*Technological advancement*
Innovation	*Results and accountability*
Enrichment	*Skill mastery*
Resourcefulness	*Teamwork*
Community	*Tolerance of differences*

Improve student achievement in the areas of graduation rate, mastery performance levels, and equity for disadvantaged students.

Enhance community relations through more effective communication, the reporting of and accountability for results, and involvement in school activities.

Promote technology with the goal of preparing students for 21st century skills, cultural literacy, virtual field trips, advanced communications, and distance learning, while ensuring all students access and integrating technology with instruction.

Support our human resources through fair contracts, a positive work environment, high expectations, recruitment and training for excellence, and by expanding our volunteer resources.

Ensure the integrity of our district finances by offering the best services within our means, seeking alternative funding sources, and developing a long-range (three to four years) financial plan.

Guiding Philosophy
Reinvention and revitalization

Figure 5.3: Strategic plan for improving student achievement.

opportunity to develop their fluency with this language for their individual practice and for their collective work and communication. Jeff understood the central role that language plays in organizations. As Bolman and Deal (1997) write in their book *Reframing Organizations,* "A specialized language both shapes and reflects a group's culture" (p. 254). Jeff was purposefully introducing a language for thinking, which all members of the school community at all levels could use to work collaboratively, communicate clearly, construct meaning together, and validate the multiple perspectives present in the system. This was foundational work on which Jeff and his colleagues would continue to build a sustainable system strengthened by the individual and collective efficacy of all members.

The idea of sustainability is rooted in the concept of ecology. Ecosystems are designed to be self-sustaining, supported, and strengthened by the interdependence and cooperation of all members. Rather than organized in hierarchies, "the web of life," writes Fritjof Capra (1996), "consists of networks within networks" (p. 35). School systems can be excellent examples of such ecosystems. While organized hierarchically, they naturally resist the artificial nature of such a structure and thrive when pathways of communication and interaction move freely between and among all members. As Capra (1996) states, "Ecological communities have been seen as consisting of organisms linked together in network fashion through feeding relations" (p. 34). They work successfully as a functional whole when adhering to the properties of interdependence and reciprocity.

Jeff Matteson had begun this process in Canisteo-Greenwood, and his colleagues joined in creating a school system that would evolve into a highly functioning ecosystem. With what Linda Lambert (2007, p. 311) refers to as "an improving image of what sustainable schools look like," Jeff and his colleagues were now deeply engaged in the hard work of making such a vision a reality. Central to this effort was addressing the question, How, then, do those in school systems feed each other and nourish the individual and collective energy of the members in order to become self-sustaining and serve their students more effectively?

Becoming a Professional Learning Community

Significantly, Canisteo-Greenwood began to explore the idea of reformulating its identity around the concept of becoming a professional learning community, which it saw as directly aligned with its strategic plan. The similarities that emerged in the Double Bubble Map the district created to compare its strategic plan to professional learning communities (PLCs) clearly indicate this (figure 5.4, page 76). To effectively reconstruct the school's identity around this concept, and to ensure the skillful participation of all members of the school community in this process, Jeff immediately associated the work Canisteo-Greenwood had begun to do with Thinking Maps with this initiative.

The community aspect of learning is a critical dimension of the conceptualization of schools as learning communities. It recognizes that knowledge is as much a social construct as it is an individual one, mediated through the interaction of ideas and experiences that people share within the community. Language is a unifying feature of a community. As a common visual language for thinking, Thinking Maps offer all members of a school community a shared way to elicit, discuss, and examine the individual and collective wisdom within the organization. They provide the community with a common tool for suppressing the impulse to arrive too quickly and superficially at a solution before fully surfacing the range of possibilities beyond those immediately evident. The interactive and dynamic use of Thinking Maps feeds the hunger of professional learning communities for looking comprehensively at the topics and challenges they must address to meet the ever-changing needs of their students. Thinking Maps inherently place trust in the ability of professional learning community members to

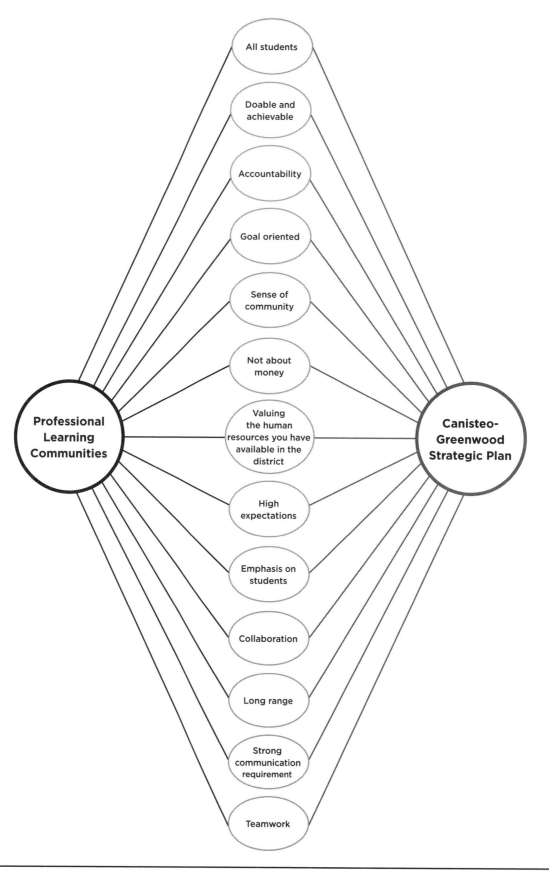

Figure 5.4: Sample Double Bubble Map comparing PLCs and a strategic school plan.

think deeply about a topic and arrive at a collective knowing and decision through a process of inquiry. Their use affirms learning as a core value of the school community. It demonstrates and places confidence in the members of the organization to arrive at meaningful and effective solutions through a genuine process of discovery and learning. The use of Thinking Maps to generate ideas, surface multiple frames of reference, and examine a topic through a variety of lenses produces rich data that inform the critical decisions to be made and the actions subsequently taken. As a common language, it empowers all members of the school to lead and participate in these critical investigative processes with skill and effectiveness.

After sending groups of teacher leaders to seminars on professional learning communities, Jeff decided to further support their efforts by engaging them in a training using Thinking Maps as tools for leadership. Already knowledgeable in the use of Thinking Maps with their students, these participants would now learn how to use Thinking Maps for facilitating meetings, establishing decision-making processes, and conducting a range of leadership practices associated with the work of building and sustaining their system as a professional learning community. The use of Thinking Maps fit seamlessly into this process. As a language for learning, the maps meaningfully supported the emphasis on inquiry. As visual models for representing the individual and collective thinking of the members of the community, the maps placed attention on the ideas, making them the central focus of the interactions—not the personalities and emotions that can often inhibit the learning process. Perhaps most importantly, the maps provided people who previously had limited opportunities to exercise and develop their leadership skills and capacities with the tools to confidently assume those roles in the context of the professional learning communities they were developing. Immediately following the Thinking Maps leadership training, one teacher contacted Jeff to share her excitement and appreciation for a professional learning experience she could instantly put into practice. Having just come from a meeting in which she and a colleague used Thinking Maps to facilitate a discussion, the teacher wrote the following.

> Jeff, what is so exciting about yesterday's workshop is that the ideas presented there were put into practice at the homework committee meeting. It was clear the direction we needed to take to start to build a frame for our homework policy. Nick allowed Tabitha and me to help run the meeting using what was learned at the Thinking Maps training. It was the difference between night and day from our first meeting to our second. All of the griping that went on during the first meeting was completely erased with a direction (not the answers, yet) and the direction included input from everyone. No one had to feel left out and unheard. This is my eighth year teaching in this district and prior to this year, I have not had the opportunity for a leadership role. There has been lots of opportunities to work in and with teams, but not the opportunity for me to step into a leadership role (and, I am so ready and appreciative of the opportunity). For example,

without the PLC/Thinking Maps training, I would not have the understand-ing and knowledge to help lead that meeting yesterday. It did seem like our committee made a step forward and I believe we will make another step forward in our next meeting. I am glad to have Nick as a principal, but I am also glad to have you as our superintendent. Again, thank you for the leader-ship opportunities, because I am ready to grow. (D. McCutcheon, personal communication with J. Matteson, December 15, 2009)

We have all been in meetings—countless, endless, and unproductive meetings—in which we feel disengaged or powerless to influence the process or the outcomes. Often these meetings lack a clear focus and any tangible outcomes. If there is a process, it is often just that—a process that goes on without resulting in coherent ideas or actions informed by the information generated. The minutes of such meetings also frequently represent one person's interpretation of the meetings' contents and outcomes and often look nothing like what various participants actually experienced.

Thinking Maps provide a clear focus and direction and naturally create the context for mean-ingful engagement and collaboration. The maps themselves form the minutes of the meeting and provide an accurate historical record of both the content and the process of the ideas discussed. The maps make it easy to reconstruct the conversation and re-enter the process at a later time. Perhaps most significantly, as this teacher's observation highlights, the professional development enabled her to develop the competencies to fulfill the role of leader, a role she had aspired to but had previously not been adequately prepared to step into. Sustainable schools require people to participate as leaders and contributors in highly effective ways. To sustain the level of engagement needed to address the complex issues that schools face, everyone involved must contribute skill-fully and constructively.

Collectively Creating a Meaningful, Sustainable Plan

The experience the teacher described was not isolated. It certainly complemented the experi-ences of Jeff and others as Jeff introduced the use of Thinking Maps in his initial work in the system. One story worth noting is from Norma Bond, a teacher leader recounting a presentation on a topic of real importance to the work within the system to meet the needs of all students in an effective and timely manner.

Imagine you're sitting in a workshop. The presenter is introducing a lot of vital information, and you and your colleagues are responsible for translating it into an action plan. The presenter uses some new terms, and the language washes over you, gently and steadily at first, until it accumu-lates and gathers speed. At that point, it begins to feel more like an unrelenting torrent, and you struggle for it not to overwhelm you. You reach out to hang onto something, a key point, perhaps, or a familiar association. Maybe you actively resist what is said, diminish its relevance and value, and hope that this, too, shall pass as have other such things before. Alternatively, overwhelmed, you simply let go, tune out, withdraw from the process, and allow yourself to be swept along and hope for the best. Sound familiar? Norma, the teacher leader, experienced this in a meeting on a major districtwide initiative.

The presenter, a leader in the field, introduced the participants to a new framework the district would be adopting for meeting students' needs. Along with the background information, those attending the session learned they would have to take this information and formulate a comprehensive plan immediately. As the presenter spoke and the words continued to flow, Norma considered her options, surveyed the expression on the faces of her colleagues, and said to the group, "We need a map!" Electing neither to sink nor resist, Norma reached instead for the tools she knew would not only prevent her and her colleagues from being engulfed by this flood of information but enable them to transform the information into actionable knowledge and a meaningful, sustainable plan. With the chart paper available, Norma and her colleagues began to use a series of Thinking Maps—a Circle Map to identify what they needed to do; a Tree Map to organize the information generated, add additional details, and assign responsibilities; another Tree Map to identify the type of information they needed to consider about students; a Flow Map to delineate the steps in the initial process; and another Flow Map to establish an agreed-on meeting protocol (figures 5.5, 5.6, and 5.7, pages 80–81). Each Thinking Map was chosen in response to a question the group was trying to answer as they thought through the RTI process. For example, the Circle Map was chosen to assist the group in answering the question, What do we need to consider as part of our RTI process?

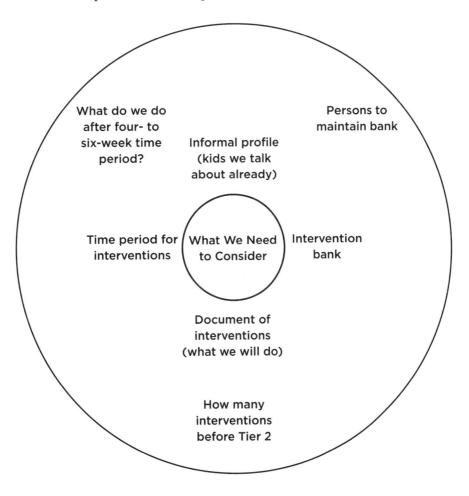

Figure 5.5: Sample Circle Map to identify what needs to be considered in the RTI process.

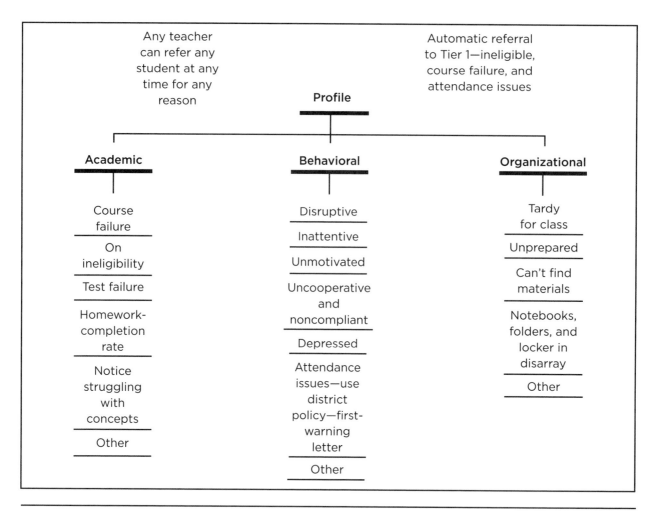

Figure 5.6: Sample Tree Map to identify different aspects of student needs.

In two hours, Norma said they transformed an experience vital to their mission but on the verge of collapsing into a meaningful plan with the support and enthusiasm of those involved. Norma noted that it was remarkable so much could be accomplished in such a short period of time on a complex topic. They accomplished this through the collective effort and thinking of the group and visually displayed maps. Acknowledging how clearly the group represented the information from his presentation, the presenter continued to invite Norma to visually represent his ideas as he introduced them to the group. Shortly after the meeting, all participants received computer-generated versions of the same maps they had created on paper during the meeting—a complete and accurate record of their discussion and decisions and the plan they would now put into place.

Achieving the systemic transformation Jeff hoped to accomplish required a multidimensional approach. Jeff's efforts centered on creating a system in which people were individually and collectively engaged in a process of continuous learning. It influenced the choices he made with the resources he had, and it guided his own actions. Jeff fully endorsed the dispositions of practice associated with professional learning communities: commitment to understanding,

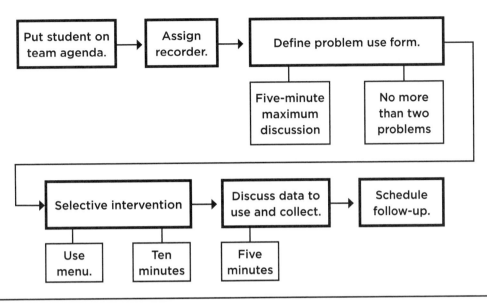

Figure 5.7: Sample Flow Map to identify the intervention meeting process.

intellectual perseverance, courage and initiative, commitment to reflection, commitment to expertise, and collegiality. With all eyes on him, Jeff genuinely and authentically modeled the skills and dispositions he hoped would come to characterize the organization as a whole. More importantly, he carefully designed a process by which members of the school community could develop the same competencies and dispositions and exercise them in situations of real importance and relevance.

Developing the Glue

Thinking Maps became the glue that connected people to each other and to the mission of the system through meaningful, purposeful interactions. As one teacher leader noted:

> *What's cool about the visual piece to this is that you can see your thinking together—it's so objective and nonjudgmental—put it on a visual display. . . . You can solve problems and make plans without it being contentious. When you're in these processes and folks have their own biases and assumptions you assume certain things. But when you plan with the maps, all this is displayed—reframes the whole way you plan with some people. The maps provide us ways to be productive with people that you might not normally be productive with.*

The use of the maps made the purpose and direction of the meetings clear to participants. The group clearly articulated the guiding questions it used to direct its inquiry on each topic. This naturally led to the group's selection of the maps that would be used to support the thinking processes as it worked to understand the issues and develop possible solutions. The thinking process evident in each question guided the group in selecting the appropriate Thinking Maps to facilitate their inquiry. The use of Thinking Maps required participants to suspend judgment and to consider how best to think about an issue. People were challenged to identify the right questions before moving too quickly to finding the right answer. Using questions and the appropriate maps opened participants to possibilities that cut across preconceived ideas and presumptions that they might have had about the topic before the collective inquiry began.

Without sacrificing the relational aspect of group process key to creating community, the use of Thinking Maps allowed the group to work efficiently and in a highly attuned manner. On a number of occasions, people reported the satisfaction of completing tasks not only in less time than normally expected but in a way that produced actions for which there was a high degree of commitment and enthusiasm. As Jeff described his interaction with the school board during a process of analyzing data, he observed:

> [The] board and administration met on a Saturday. . . . They never took a break, they were so into it—all were contributing, everything was positive and moving forward and at the end of the ten maps we had all the content we needed for this one-page document. . . . In three hours and twenty minutes we had a five-year strategic plan of goals and core values.

The process of using Thinking Maps produced meaningful information that the group used to inform future actions. Decision steps were embedded in a coherent process without the risk of becoming disconnected.

One of the principals echoed Jeff's observations describing her use of the maps with her school's response to intervention (RTI) steering committee. She said, "I told the steering committee that this was my first time doing this." Together they decided what Thinking Maps to use to facilitate the conversation. Looking back on the experience, the principal remarked, "I couldn't believe how smoothly it went—I was thinking I didn't have enough time to get through everything but it just went smoothly. . . . It was very easy for everyone to be engaged in the process."

Another principal offered these observations about the effectiveness of the maps following their use in designing an end-of-the-year orientation process for teachers new to the district with a team of veteran teachers:

> We had a lot of people around the table for that planning process—there is a computer and a SMART Board and Thinking Maps software. We did a Circle Map, then a Flow Map with the steps, and then a Tree Map for the different parts of the training. We had the process on the software.

Noting that the time of year for this meeting was not necessarily optimal for its success, the principal commented, "The next-to-the-last day of school, sometimes folks are checking out, but when you have the maps as part of the planning document—the discussions are more focused; they can see it and stay focused." The visual element of the maps holds people's attention. However, their effectiveness clearly goes beyond simply attention grabbing. The principal added:

> *It seems like everyone's needs are met. . . . When you see this and everyone's ideas are put up on a map everyone feels listened to and their ideas heard—facilitates more thought—no dead time, but people are visualizing what's on the maps and then processing and the light switch goes on and more ideas come out. So we come out with ten to twenty good ideas versus four to five.*

When working with visually accessible information that includes the ideas of all stakeholders, the principal observed that people are "more interested in finding a solution."

Experiences such as these build momentum and organizational confidence. One senior administrator offered the following observation: "I feel a lot better where we're headed. . . . Now we can see there is a direction and a purpose. We know what we're doing, we can see the path, and we're ready to go—and how we're going to get there." Another administrator added:

> *The focus has always been on surviving fiscally and dealing with those issues—this feels like the first year that we've had a direction and focus on education and learning. Now we know the path and process and everyone is behind that and ready to go. From all staff everyone was looking for that direction—where are we headed now?*

Clearly, people in Canisteo-Greenwood feel energized and empowered. They are also as deeply committed to the direction the superintendent has developed as he is. Commenting on this, one member of the leadership team emphatically stated, "I work at it because it is so important to Jeff and important to our school that we follow through."

With each success, the individuals within the organization grow in their optimism and perception of the system's ability to address the most complicated situations. Surely these will arise. However, in an organization in which the skills of effective leadership have been carefully developed and distributed and in which value has been placed on collegiality and community and supported in tangible ways, the prospect for ongoing success and sustained growth and development is strong. Canisteo-Greenwood is well on its way to becoming such a system.

Schoolwide Thinking

Joseph Campbell observed in an interview that we often tell and retell stories, not to explain things, but to return to the experience. With each retelling of the same story, something new emerges—a crystallizing, perhaps, of the central meaning or meanings that exist within it but require the retelling in order to take form and surface. Our interviews with educators using Thinking Maps for their leadership practices invited them to go back into those experiences, retell them, and identify new learning and insights. From these interviews—the retelling of important, and sometimes intense, high-stakes experiences about shifts and changes across whole schools—major themes emerged.

It's interesting to note that in the experiences described to us, the people involved used Thinking Maps to facilitate the surfacing of their own and each other's ideas. In a sense, the maps became tools for visually telling and retelling the story of the experiences as well as representing the internal dialogue of each person's own thinking. They became vehicles for surfacing meaning, making connections, and formulating actions, because as we know, the brain constantly maps external experiences and remembers meaningful moments with the connective patterns of neurons. One school leader commented, "Thinking Maps have particularly helped me to be work smart when planning strategically in order to get ideas down on paper before deciding and moving forward."

In the integration of several different stories in this chapter, we see that transforming a whole school is possible when a language for surfacing thinking becomes the connective tissue between and among people, some of whom don't work directly with each other or even across the hall on a day-to-day basis. We can also begin to hear and see how educators who use the maps for their own personal-professional problem solving—in coaching and one-to-one contexts, or even in small-group meetings—are engaged at a new level after seeing Thinking Maps used across a whole community of learners and leaders. They experience, in the practice of using Thinking Maps, that the whole is greater than the parts as we weave the patterns of thinking together to bring clarity to complex situations without making difficult choices simple or distorting ideas to fit immediate needs.

In these retellings, the themes of clarity, efficiency, collaboration, empowerment, and sustainability emerged, and respondents expressed them explicitly. Clarity, in particular, continually surfaced as a theme when people were asked to identify the contributions Thinking Maps made to their leadership practice. Many of those interviewed expressed this explicitly as *clarity* and also provided related statements about transparency, coherence, and purposefulness. One teacher leader observed, "It helps me visualize my thoughts so I can convey them succinctly." An elementary principal commented, "The Thinking Maps force me to focus, [force me to] be specific, and make me a better planner and questioner." Lastly, as elementary school Principal Judy Kantor explained when working through a particularly difficult interaction with a teacher, "The Thinking Maps make things very clear in my mind and allow me to articulate it [the thinking] very well."

The phrase "I see what you mean" could be adapted to express "I see what I mean." Both phrases represent the value of using Thinking Maps for helping people understand the meaning and intent of others' ideas and to become more precise and clear about their own thinking. Dickmann and Stanford-Blair (2002) identify the brain's capacity for consciousness, an awareness of self in relationship to others, as an evolutionary breakthrough that "enabled reflection about probabilities, possibilities, and options" (p. 126). For the individuals involved in this study, Thinking Maps supported and enhanced the brain's ability to function optimally and consequently choose actions that positively influenced the individuals' interactions with others. Evidently, too, the confidence, borne of the clarity people developed in the process of using Thinking Maps to formulate and communicate their thinking, fundamentally altered their stance in relationship to others regardless of role, thus impacting the culture of the organization.

Networks of Learning Relationships

The presence of these five themes in each of the previous case studies and in our interviews and surveys of school leaders was not limited to particular roles. Apparently, the ground on which people stood shifted when leaders introduced Thinking Maps as a language for educators in adult interactions as well as for young people in the context of student learning. A notable benefit of the use of the maps for leadership practices and organizational communication was its impact on the conceptualization of individual roles and relationships across the entire school community. Ken McGuire, principal of Bluebonnet Elementary School in Texas, described Thinking Maps' impact on his work and his school in this way:

> As far as my leadership, I continue to work to create effective communication and collaboration, help generate shared mission and vision, conduct meaningful and purposeful professional growth, direct problem-solving strategies, collect and analyze information, and manage the business of the campus. Thinking Maps have made me more effective in these areas. I now have a set of tools that establish a common language and help the staff recognize the kind of thinking we are doing. The maps provide process and help define purpose in the work of our teams and committees. (K. McGuire, personal communication, March 2, 2009)

Process and *purpose*, the dual benefits from using Thinking Maps for leadership practices that Ken identified, connect directly to the themes of collaboration, clarity, and efficiency. Sustaining the engagement of faculty members in a change process can be directly linked to how meaningful they perceive the activities associated with it to be. As Michael Fullan (2001b) observes, "Purposeful interaction is essential for continuous improvement" across a learning community (p. 124).

The ability to facilitate such processes is critical to how a leader's effectiveness is perceived and the degree to which a leader, leadership teams, and connective, distributed leadership will succeed in eliciting meaningful contributions from faculty. However, if only the titled or formally identified leader—the principal, for example—is adept at conducting interactions in this way, the culture remains hierarchically bound and paternalistic. Top-down leadership is from a time gone by, but leadership solely from the ground up can be equally detrimental. Another place must be found where flexible, coherent structures for high-quality thinking and communication can be consciously practiced and not be determined by role or position within the organization. Lambert (2009) asserts that when reciprocal structures are lacking, "the result is disengagement; apathy; and retreat into focus on the self, prejudice, and fear" (p. 11). Certainly, this is not a recipe for successful organizational improvement or individual growth.

Ken McGuire understood this and committed to developing a professional learning community that valued and empowered teachers and thus empowered him in a rich reciprocal, virtuous, and sustainable feedback loop. He said emphatically, "I learned that no school structure creates success for students unless it is founded on a climate that values and empowers the teachers who serve those students, and provides teachers with the tools and facilitation they need to do their job effectively." Ken intuitively grasped what Dorothy Cohen (1973), a former senior faculty member of the Bank Street College Graduate School of Education, articulated years earlier when she observed:

> *Our educational system will not change until both teachers and children are perceived as human beings. Only a self-respecting, accepted, autonomous teacher, proud of her professional integrity, can relate to children in ways that will give children self-respect, acceptance, autonomy, and pride in their accomplishments. (p. 23)*

Through Ken's guidance, Thinking Maps became a common visual language throughout Bluebonnet's campus; all members of the school community used them for all purposes associated with educating students. This included the collaborative work of the adults in improving their instructional practices (figures 6.1 and 6.2, pages 88–89), solving problems, addressing challenges, and making decisions critical to the successful fulfillment of the school's mission (figure 6.3, page 90). The Flow Map in figure 6.1, for example, highlights Bluebonnet Elementary School teachers' effective use of this map to guide them in formulating the questions they needed to address as they considered the implementation of the Daily 5, a literacy strategy designed to engage students in activities to improve reading and writing skills. Each of the questions they identified would promote discussion and be supported by the appropriate map. The group generated the ideas in the Frame of Reference to keep in mind factors that would influence their thinking as they responded to the questions.

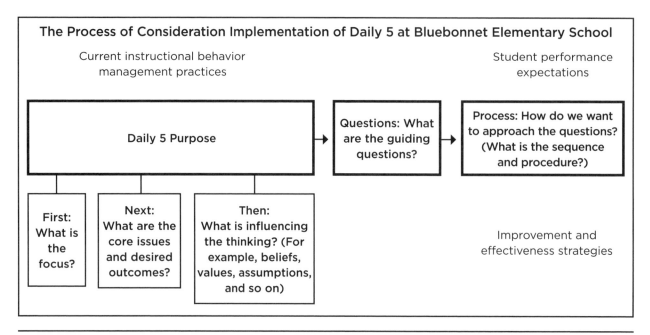

Figure 6.1: Sample Flow Map for instructional practice implementation.

Ken's use of Thinking Maps and his recognition of the importance of extending the use of these tools to all members of the school community fundamentally transformed the organizational environment. The reciprocal, purposeful interactions fostered by the use of Thinking Maps reframed the school's structure from one based on hierarchies to a "network of learning relationships" (Lambert, 2009, p. 9)—the essence of connective thinking and leading. Ken and his colleagues were deeply engaged in the process Lambert (2009) characterizes as "leading as a form of learning" (p. 9). Ken reflects, "We are still developing as a Thinking Maps environment, but each day we learn more ways to employ them as the conduit through which the learning and the business of our campus flows. *As an entire school community we are learning to think!*" [italics added].

Thinking Maps, Thinking Teams, Thinking Students, Thinking Schools

Let's investigate several schools where Thinking Maps became an unwitting catalyst for strengthening schoolwide leadership and increasing communication that also led directly to improved student learning outcomes. First, we consider the insights from a vertical team at Florence E. Blackham School in Bridgeport, Connecticut, where the maps had just been introduced the year before, and then those from Yates Mill Elementary School, in the research triangle of North Carolina, where Thinking Maps had been used as a language for students and teachers for over eight years. Both sites engaged in yearlong action research specifically focused on leadership with Thinking Maps as they became aware of the shift in how their schools were transforming.

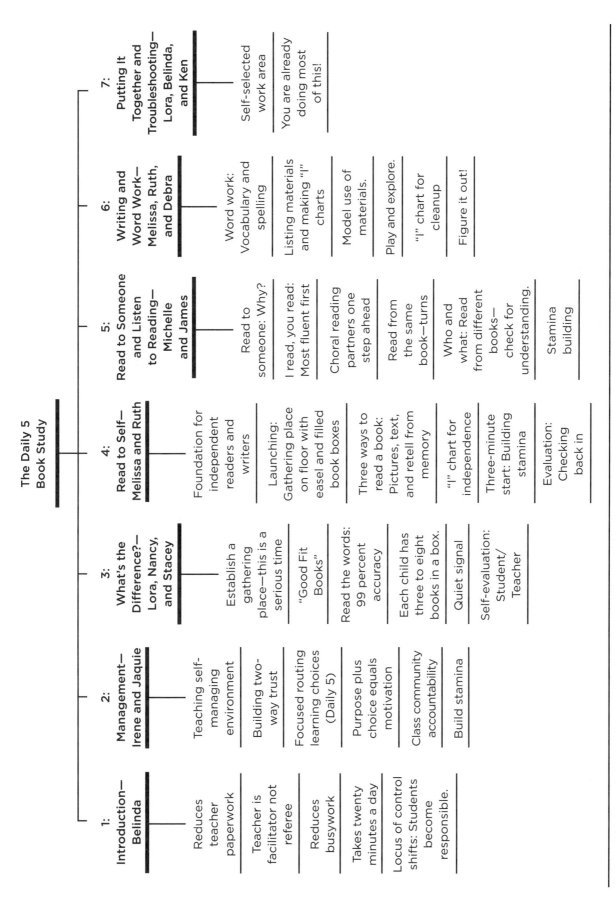

The Daily 5 Book Study

1: Introduction— Belinda
- Reduces teacher paperwork
- Teacher is facilitator not referee
- Reduces busywork
- Takes twenty minutes a day
- Locus of control shifts: Students become responsible.

2: Management— Irene and Jaquie
- Teaching self-managing environment
- Building two-way trust
- Focused routing learning choices (Daily 5)
- Purpose plus choice equals motivation
- Class community accountability
- Build stamina

3: What's the Difference?— Lora, Nancy, and Stacey
- Establish a gathering place—this is a serious time
- "Good Fit Books"
- Read the words: 99 percent accuracy
- Each child has three to eight books in a box.
- Quiet signal
- Self-evaluation: Student/ Teacher

4: Read to Self— Melissa and Ruth
- Foundation for independent readers and writers
- Launching: Gathering place on floor with easel and filled book boxes
- Three ways to read a book: Pictures, text, and retell from memory
- "I" chart for independence
- Three-minute start: Building stamina
- Evaluation: Checking back in

5: Read to Someone and Listen to Reading— Michelle and James
- Read to someone: Why?
- I read, you read: Most fluent first
- Choral reading partners one step ahead
- Read from the same book—turns
- Who and what: Read from different books— check for understanding.
- Stamina building

6: Writing and Word Work— Melissa, Ruth, and Debra
- Word work: Vocabulary and spelling
- Listing materials and making "I" charts
- Model use of materials.
- Play and explore.
- "I" chart for cleanup
- Figure it out!

7: Putting It Together and Troubleshooting— Lora, Belinda, and Ken
- Self-selected work area
- You are already doing most of this!

Figure 6.2: Sample Tree Map for book study.

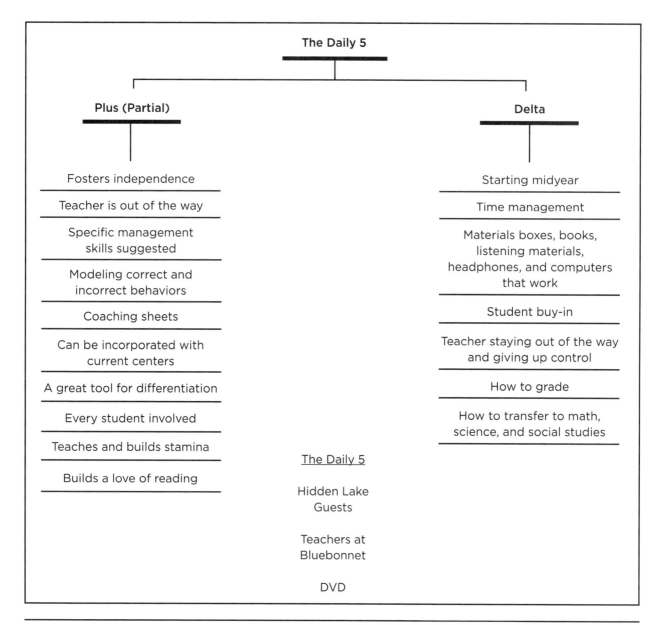

Figure 6.3: Sample Tree Map for the school mission.

A Language for Analysis and Reflection

In response to a series of statewide initiatives and in support of its efforts to improve student performance, the faculty at Blackham School undertook the formation of both horizontal and vertical data teams and the creation of processes for meaningfully and collaboratively engaging teachers in gathering, organizing, and analyzing data to improve instruction and student learning. The formation of the grade-level Horizontal Data Teams was a first step toward complying with the Connecticut Accountability for Learning Initiative (CALI), the statewide model of continuous school and district improvement that was created to close Connecticut's achievement gaps. The next step was the formation of the schoolwide Vertical Data Team. This team of teachers was responsible for data analysis and instructional and curricula decision making. It comprised teacher leaders from each grade level and content area (representing prekindergarten through grade 8), the numeracy coach, literacy coaches, and the middle school's English as a second-language teacher. Members of this team noted that while no administrators were represented on the team itself, their active support of the team's work was critical to its success (Thinking Foundation, n.d.d).

Commenting on the early stages of this process, team members shared the following observation in their research report after following the protocols that the consultants from the Connecticut State Department of Education recommended.

> *These initial meetings included quite a bit of thoughtful discussion and the presenting of ideas and opinions on student achievement at our school. At times members left meetings with their own take on the discussion, leaving much to interpretation. By the next meeting, we relied on the summarization caught by the recorder as well as our own individual recollections. The need for a system that would allow the Vertical Data Team to capture these ideas and to arrange them in powerful, more visible ways in order to be more productive was evident. (Thinking Foundation, n.d.d)*

A visiting educator, after observing a Vertical Data Team meeting, suggested that members consider using Thinking Maps to facilitate their interactions and the analysis of the data gathered. Having already seen the positive impact of the maps on student learning and communication within the classroom over the past year, the team decided to act on this suggestion with the hope "that use of the maps would lead to deeper discussions, increased participation of members, clearer goals, and improved efficiency within the Vertical Team, with the added benefit of a trickle-down effect to the Horizontal Data Teams" (Thinking Foundation, n.d.d).

As the foundation for the whole-school change effort, the Vertical Data Team decided to use Thinking Maps as a common visual language for the critical work of leading their school's commitment to continuous improvement. As a result, the team experienced the direct impact of this use of Thinking Maps for leadership purposes on several key areas of this effort: distributive leadership, communication, and student learning outcomes.

Distributive Leadership

Collaborative processes and the concept of *service leadership* were introduced into the Bridgeport Public Schools as part of an initiative to value and promote a professional attitude and improve communication. This initiative attempted primarily to expand the use of the talents, expertise, and commitment of the faculty members to deepen their involvement in decision making. The horizontal and vertical team structure at Blackham School was already aligned with the service leadership model's goal of building social capital throughout schools. However, the school would determine how to implement this model. Since all teachers were already familiar with Thinking Maps as an instructional tool, the team decided to use them for its collaborative processes. As a first step, the team members used a Circle Map to define their mission (figure 6.4) (Thinking Foundation, n.d.d).

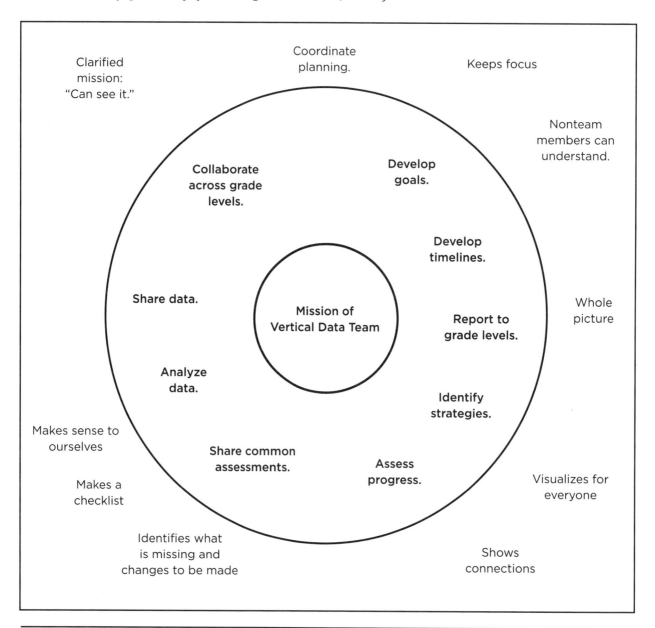

Figure 6.4: Sample Circle Map to define the school's mission.

In the Frame surrounding the ideas the team generated, members reflected on the process and identified specific ways in which the use of the Circle Map contributed to this effort. The team identified clarity and engagement—the ability to visualize the whole picture and *see* the patterns in order to make the necessary, important connections—as significant contributions, enabling all members of the school community not on the team to see and understand the ideas.

From this Circle Map, the Vertical Data Team formulated its mission statement.

The mission of the Blackham School Vertical Data Team is to collaborate schoolwide, share and analyze data, create common assessments, impart strategies, and develop timelines to achieve set goals in coordination with Horizontal Data Teams. (Thinking Foundation, n.d.d)

The success the group experienced with this initial application inspired its members to develop an action research project (with support from the Thinking Foundation) with the expectation that the proposal would allow them "to examine the ways in which using Thinking Maps as a leadership tool could support the development of distributive leadership skills and improved communication in the service of increasing student outcomes" (Thinking Foundation, n.d.d). Because the use of Thinking Maps coincided with the beginning of this collaborative structure, the maps became the primary language, or common set of tools, for deeper, visual thinking. The group immediately felt the impact of their use:

[Thinking Maps] enabled us to organize the overwhelming amount of ideas and thoughts generated by a team of twenty-two people. The beneficial focus of our action research project facilitated the inquiry and discussion of real problems facing the Vertical Data Team and their solutions. (Thinking Foundation, n.d.d)

With the maps, teachers—some with limited leadership experience—could participate in and actually facilitate collaborative processes in skillful ways. The group and its individual members developed confidence in their ability to use the vertical team structure efficiently and effectively to address the complex task of transforming data into meaningful instructional decisions for the school.

Using Thinking Maps quickly began to fulfill a variety of logistical and analytical purposes. During their team meetings, for example, the educators began by using Flow Maps to form the agenda (Thinking Foundation, n.d.d). (See figure 6.5, page 94.)

The team used other maps to:

- Define and set goals (Circle Map, Tree Map)
- Schedule and assign team tasks (Flow Map, Tree Map)
- Communicate data (Tree Map, Double Bubble Map)
- Generate ideas (Circle Map, Tree Map, Bubble Map)

After using Thinking Maps to define its mission and then to identify specific goals, the Vertical Data Team continued its reflective process and decided to explicitly address the question, What would the causes and effects be if our Vertical Data Team functioned at a high

Blackham School Vertical Data Team Agenda June 1, 2009

```
┌──────────┐    ┌──────────┐    ┌──────────────┐    ┌──────────────┐
│ Call to  │ →  │ Celebrate.│ → │ Introduce new │ → │ Horizontal and│
│  order.  │    │          │    │ members to    │    │ Vertical      │
│          │    │          │    │ the team for  │    │ Data Team     │
│          │    │          │    │ next school   │    │ binders       │
│          │    │          │    │ year.         │    │               │
└──────────┘    └──────────┘    └──────────────┘    └──────────────┘

┌──────────────┐    ┌──────────────┐    ┌──────────────┐
│ Decide what  │ →  │ Create       │ →  │ Pick two     │
│ to include.  │    │ schedule of  │    │ challenges   │
│              │    │ dates for    │    │ to focus on  │
│              │    │ 2009 to      │    │ next school  │
│              │    │ 2010 school  │    │ year.        │
│              │    │ year.        │    │              │
└──────────────┘    └──────────────┘    └──────────────┘

┌──────────────┐    ┌──────────────┐
│ Choose date  │ →  │ Next-steps   │
│ of last      │    │ parking lot  │
│ meeting and  │    │              │
│ luncheon.    │    │              │
└──────────────┘    └──────────────┘
```

Figure 6.5: Sample Flow Map for a team's agenda.

level? Posing this question and using a Multi-Flow Map to generate responses enabled the team members to formulate a clear sense of purpose for how to effectively achieve their goals and fulfill their mission—and identify what it would look and sound like if they did (Thinking Foundation, n.d.d). (See figure 6.6.)

Encouraged by their success in the Vertical Data Team context, the Blackham School Vertical Data Team members were now determined to expand the proficient use of Thinking Maps within the Horizontal Data Teams to deepen discussion, increase the efficient working of the teams through the active participation of their members, and set clearer goals. They commented, "We expect these actions to foster the growth of more social capital within the building" (Thinking Foundation, n.d.d).

Communication

The professional development the Vertical Data Team members received in Thinking Maps specifically focused on leadership applications, along with their previous exposure to the work in the classroom context, proved useful as they progressed toward using the maps as a common visual language to communicate ideas and multiple points of view. This is important to highlight: *the same language for learning across the school became a language for leading thinking across the school.* Once the Vertical Data Team members had determined they would use Thinking Maps to support their efforts to pattern information and see interconnections between ideas, they continued with increased confidence to tackle the more complex tasks of formulating their mission statement and putting it in motion:

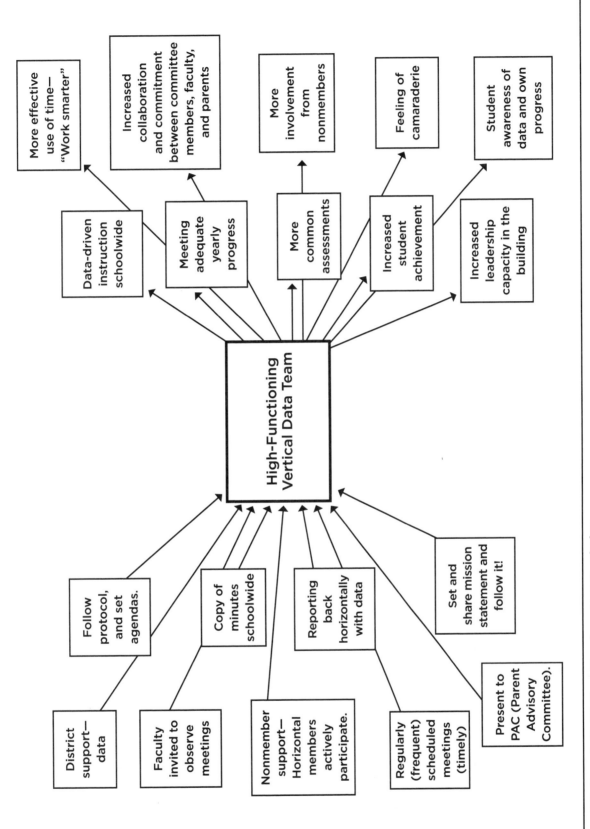

Figure 6.6: Sample Multi-Flow Map for a team's mission.

- *Recording* their schoolwide SMART goals

- *Displaying* their progress in reaching those goals

- *Communicating* those findings openly with various Blackham School stakeholders: teachers, students, staff, parents, community members, and any other individuals concerned about the success of their students

The Vertical Data Team was charged with the task of analyzing Connecticut Mastery Test (CMT) data and determining the areas that were cause for celebration or concern. The results of these common formative assessments were displayed as they related to progress toward the school's SMART goals (goals that are strategic and specific, measurable, attainable, results based, and timebound for reading and math) with a Tree Map. This simple format allowed all staff and visitors to see on one page the full array of areas of strengths as well as challenges and to look for patterns across grade levels. Prior to using the maps, the team relied solely on the minutes of the previous meetings for data recollection and further communications with other schoolwide stakeholders. As the team members explained, "Each Horizontal Data Team had shared its common formative assessment [CFA] results using different formats, such as bar graphs, pie graphs, and numerical percentages." The use of a Tree Map enabled the teams to display data uniformly, with each grade level and content area's data for CFAs visible in one large data wall (Thinking Foundation, n.d.d).

All of the stakeholders could readily view and access the information in the data wall, located in their conference or resource room. However, unlike a wall that can be experienced as a barrier, the uniform display of the data using Thinking Maps supported people's ability to see the big picture, something the team felt had been missing from its previous processes. Transparency occurred not only in the presentation of the information but also in the manner in which the maps enabled people to see through and across data points and make connections. The team achieved its goal of having people use a common visual language to pattern information and link ideas as they processed the information individually and collectively. The visual and cognitive nature of the maps allowed for clear communication of the information and made the opportunity to identify trends more apparent and possible. A simultaneity in the *seeing* and *thinking* about the data is unique to the language of Thinking Maps.

Learning Outcomes

In our work with Thinking Maps across many educational settings, administrators frequently talk about the unintended or unforeseen effects of the implementation of the maps. Many report that while their initial intent was to directly impact student performance, deeper, more lasting changes have occurred. Stefanie Holzman, former principal of Roosevelt Elementary School in Long Beach, California, expresses it this way:

> What I didn't realize and could not foresee were the deeper effects on the development of teachers. . . . I discovered that from an administrator's point of view, Thinking Maps did much more than what I had understood from both

practical and theoretical points of view . . . there have been shifts in the culture and climate of our school, most obvious in the quality of professional conversations that now rise to the surface. (Holzman, 2011, p. 119)

Interestingly, the Vertical Data Team at Blackham School elected to use Thinking Maps for leadership purposes to *intentionally* create the very same shift that Holzman describes as an unanticipated by-product of using Thinking Maps in the classroom. The Blackham School team discovered through its efforts, however, that the leadership use of Thinking Maps had the unintended consequence of improving instruction in the classroom while promoting skillful participation among faculty in the leadership of the school. They reported:

The use of the Thinking Maps as a leadership tool in our Vertical Data Team has both directly and indirectly affected student learning outcomes at Blackham School. For example, the discussions fostered by the use of the Maps have allowed teacher-leaders to share effective instructional strategies. When our Vertical Data Team brainstormed effective strategies to support our Reading and Math SMART goals, we displayed them in a Circle Map, which was then shared with the Horizontal Data Team. Those teams added additional ideas to the map. By compiling detailed examples of these strategies and lessons in a binder, teachers will be able to access what they and their colleagues have determined to be the most effective strategies to attain our school's academic goals, providing them a way to expand their teaching repertoire without resorting to the tendency to "go it alone" and "reinvent the wheel." With increased use of these effective strategies, we expect to see an increased student achievement in our targeted areas. (Thinking Foundation, n.d.d)

The Vertical Data Team described an additional benefit: the increased use of Thinking Maps as a leadership tool in the Vertical Data Team and Horizontal Data Team led to an increase of their use in the classroom. With improved familiarity and a greater degree of fluency, teachers and students were using the maps in more complex and independent ways. Not only did use of the maps help students unite in using common strategies, but the wide variety of maps for student learning and as higher-order thinking tools also provided teachers with the means for automatic differentiation for all learners. As one teacher noted:

[Thinking Maps] not only provide continuity and structure, but also allow students to maintain focus on the task at hand, providing them with the ability to collect, organize and process information. Students can make use of maps on various subject matter and topics and interchange them within cross-curricular activities. They are valuable in providing the students with a sense of feeling confident in their academic achievements. (Thinking Foundation, n.d.d)

The use of Thinking Maps influenced learning at all levels of the school community—faculty as well as students. For members of the faculty, the use of the maps for professional interactions significantly impacted the confidence and dexterity with which they could use the maps with their students. Their growing comfort in using the maps for complex processes as part of their data-team interactions emboldened them to expand their use in the classroom, just as their students' use of the maps allowed them to approach learning with greater confidence and enthusiasm.

A final benefit that the Vertical Data Team reported once again echoed the observations that Stefanie Holzman (2011) made regarding the change in the professional discourse she observed in her school. The principal investigators for Blackham noted:

> Other benefits have been achieved through increased reflection between teachers and coaches. Interpreting classroom data with another professional not directly connected with the students can help teachers gain a new perspective as they strive to determine what might be the most effective instructional practices for the desired learning outcomes. (Thinking Foundation, n.d.d)

For the teacher leaders at Blackham School, Thinking Maps were not simply a convenient way to visually display information. They promoted a *collaborative process* that fully engaged their intellects, developed their leadership skills, and enabled them to achieve their ultimate goal of improving student learning. As a final observation, they said:

> We are encouraged by the growth of our strong professional learning community, empowering teachers as leaders via the Vertical Data Team, and initiating the use of Thinking Maps as a strategy to organize and communicate goals and objectives for the school. We feel the maps have helped drive instruction and have had a direct impact on student learning. (Thinking Foundation, n.d.d)

"Out of the Auditory": A New Kind of Meeting

When asked to identify how Thinking Maps have impacted her staff's interactions with her and each other, Lynn Williams, principal of Yates Mill Elementary School in Wake County, North Carolina, stated, "Staff meetings are fundamentally different. The use of maps makes us more objective—*out of the auditory.*" We could easily have mistaken such an interesting phrase for the more familiar "out of the ordinary." In fact, Lynn's intended meaning was the same regardless of how we heard it. She described how people get lost in the emotional sound of words, losing "sight" of the goals and reasons for their actions and focusing instead on each other. Without the visual, Lynn pointed out, hidden assumptions and misunderstandings are more likely to alter the conversation and influence the decision-making process. Most (ordinary) meetings, she observed, are dominantly auditory and, as a result, are particularly vulnerable to miscommunication and a lack of clarity. "A climate of a school is often rated by the nondiscuss-ables—we don't have these misinterpretations," Lynn noted. "When a school has good communication, you don't necessarily know it. But when a school does *not* have good communication, you *know* it." Good communication, Lynn concluded, is not just about creating a friendly atmosphere. It allows teachers to "put their brain power to teaching and learning."

At Yates Mill, educators have used Thinking Maps for over six years as a foundation for high-quality teaching and learning and occasionally for communication and leadership practices. The past few years saw a much more explicit use of the maps for improving communication, problem solving, and decision making during meetings. Using Thinking Maps in meetings allowed the faculty to examine trends, identify patterns, and keep focused on the goal. The maps made the data more readily discernible and thus enabled the faculty to make more data-informed decisions. Lynn observed, "Teachers do a better job responding when the information is easily accessible." She wanted teachers to see where things connected, something she said a Tree Map, for example, enabled them to do quite readily. "In a map," she noted, "you can see the information immediately. More information can be processed and retrieved quickly and the data can be used efficiently and effectively." Lynn described a meeting in which the faculty was planning the implementation of the Daily 5 reading program. "We asked the questions, created a Flow Map, then a Tree Map grouping where the materials were. We have all these materials. Students need books and teachers wanted to make sure they had enough books."

Teachers needed to decide where to begin the implementation. They began the process with a Flow Map, retracing the steps leading to the decision to implement the Daily 5 and reminding themselves of their intended purpose. Then, Lynn added, they constructed a Tree Map, identifying all the places where the materials were located. One teacher proposed distributing the books to the first graders. Sensing the prematurity of this solution, Lynn drew their attention back to the information in the maps they had created:

> I reminded the group that the reason we were distributing these books is that they [students] need to have a lot of books to read. I said let's decide deliberately. We looked at the Tree Map and what folks were assigned to do at each grade level and decided to start with the newest teachers. We had a plan.

By returning teachers' attention to the maps and objectifying their intended purpose, Lynn enabled the group to see patterns that might otherwise have been less apparent. She observed, "By the time the faculty walked out of the meeting with Tree Map in hand, it was clear what each person's job was and the next steps. There was no ambiguity—they had it down."

Thinking in Maps

This use of Thinking Maps for leadership practices that Lynn modeled so effectively was transferred to the teacher leaders she worked with at Yates Mill. One such teacher leader described her "aha!" moment in the use of Thinking Maps for her responsibilities as a leader of a Vertical Data Team meeting that occurred at a summer faculty retreat. Although she had noticed many opportunities to use the maps to explain different processes related to instructional initiatives the faculty had been discussing, not until she had to communicate information to her colleagues did she experience the value of this use of Thinking Maps:

> I was typing the minutes as I had done for previous meetings I had with teams and thought this was the perfect opportunity to display the information in Thinking Maps instead of my usual form of capturing what was being said at the meetings.

She began the Vertical Data Team meeting with a Circle Map (figure 6.7) to record people's expectations for these meetings, new to their school.

Figure 6.7: Sample Circle Map to record meeting expectations.

This simple act of putting pen to paper, of actually constructing a Thinking Map in the moment, secured the use of these tools in her mind and in her practice. Lynn described, "From there I just kept thinking in maps. It was *natural* to go into a Tree Map to display the successes and challenges at each grade level." (See figure 6.8.)

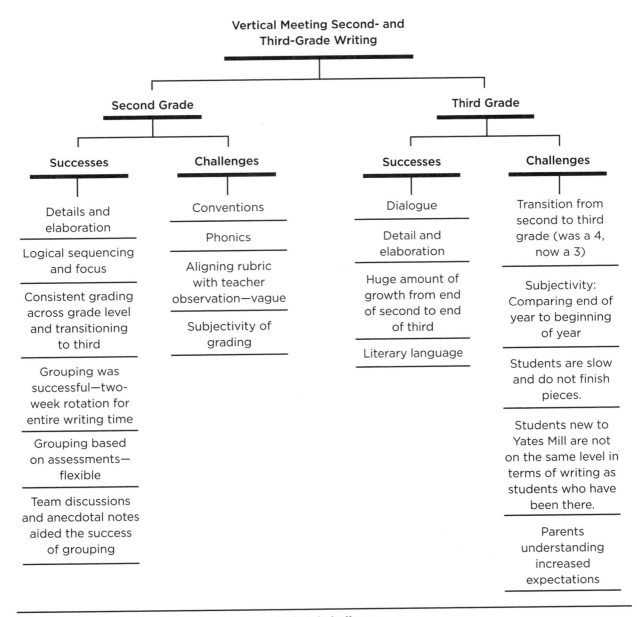

Figure 6.8: Sample Tree Map to analyze grade-level challenges.

As discussions developed from the use of maps, Lynn realized which other maps and, more precisely, which thinking processes, would support the group members in developing a deeper understanding of a particular topic. For example, after members of the third- and fourth-grade team completed their Tree Map using student work samples to help identify the successes and challenges of implementing a guided-reading approach at each grade level, they constructed a Double Bubble Map to compare the results from the two grade levels to see what patterns would emerge (figure 6.9).

Commenting on the impact this had on the group, Lynn observed, "It came naturally and the teachers responded well to that as opposed to just a couple of pages of minutes of what had been said." As for its impact on her skills as a teacher leader, she noted, "Now, when I'm discussing or planning things with other leaders or teachers, I naturally think in Thinking Maps."

Developing Empowerment

Because Thinking Maps are rooted in the application of cognitive skills fundamental to developing meaning and understanding, inquiry processes are ideally suited for their use. The professional learning community setting, where groups of educators collaborate in pursuit of understanding student learning and developing effective instructional practices, is enhanced when Thinking Maps are used as a common language among participants. "Thinking Maps give us a structure so that we can problem solve together," Lynn commented. "We ask questions, and the analysis we do is very deliberate and purposeful." Such interactions are, by their very nature, empowering for the group as well as the individuals involved. Uncertainty about a situation becomes an opportunity for learning. The maps provide a common language and a tool for faculty to engage thoughtfully and confidently in pursuit of understanding. Importantly, because no set sequence exists for using the maps, and we often use multiple maps together, this common language becomes a natural extension of fundamental patterns of thinking writ large within the distributive, connective practices of leading thinking across the whole school. Recalling the first time she participated in Thinking Maps training, another teacher leader at Yates Mill excitedly observed, "This is what my brain does. This is a picture of what happens in my brain when I encounter information."

The maps add to and are different from some more traditional and effective normed meeting processes that often become stale and clunky because they lack dynamic flexibility related to surfacing creative and analytic thinking in the moment. As this teacher began to use the maps in collaborative processes, she commented on team meetings in which participants used the maps to facilitate interactions: "Everybody comes away with a clear, common picture of what we're experiencing versus just their own stories when they leave the room." Reflecting on the impact of this use of Thinking Maps on her development as a leader, she added, "This has been a powerful way for me to grow in a direction . . . from real comfort zone with students to more comfort zone with having adult conversations in the workplace."

For Lynn, the use of Thinking Maps in these collaborative group settings represented an opportunity to provide the type of leadership she aspired to in her work. She noted, "The part I love the most is the use of the maps in working with groups with the emotional baggage." Leading a team to be empowered, she explained, can help move it beyond the dysfunction that emotions such as anxiety and fear can create. She said, "I love doing the problem solving all together and walking out with an outcome that everyone understands and is invested in."

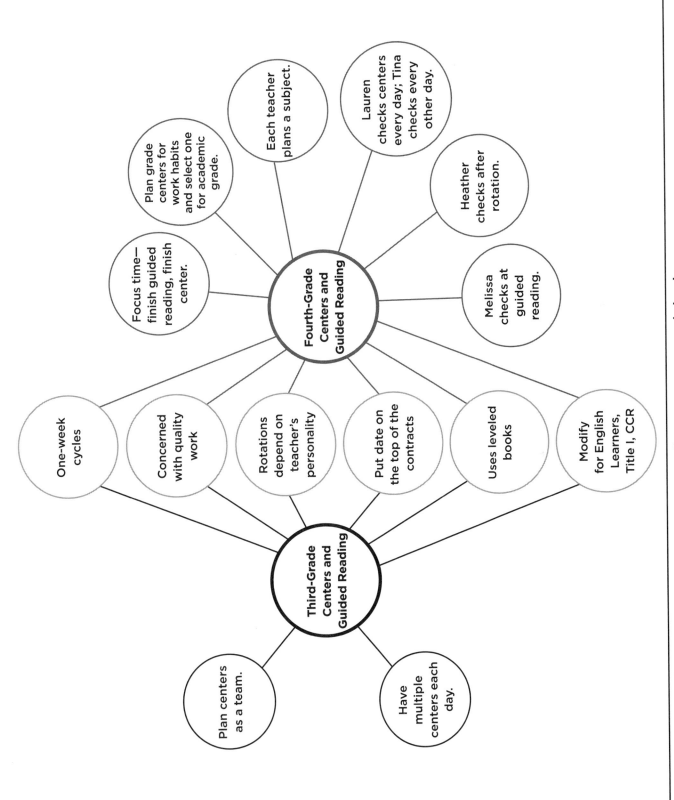

Figure 6.9: Sample Double Bubble Map to analyze guided-reading program per grade level.

Notice that *empowerment*, one of the five themes threading through these stories, is not derived by distributing roles and new responsibilities to people, or by making sure that everyone has his or her say. It develops instead through the openness of thinking within a dynamic, common language that supports individuals and groups to show their points of view within the context of deep patterns of thinking. Narrowly formulated, rational arguments from a single point of view are no longer adequate or reflective of the individual and collective potential of the people within the school community. Thus, the themes of *clarity* and *collaboration* heighten, engage, and emancipate the internal power of the mind from the small-minded conflicts that often arise in heated engagements between faculty members and within the much larger school community of parents and other interested parties.

Lynn described a meeting that occurred on the last day of school and that became quite heated. In this meeting, she experienced how the use of Thinking Maps could not only rescue a meeting from devolving into a battle of wills and accusations but transform it into an experience in which everyone involved, including herself, felt empowered and effective.

> *I had a team I brought in and said we have to think about how we're delivering gifted math services. We sat down, it was the last day of school—I let people dump all of their emotional issues. Some had axes to grind. After the first emotional dump—that "wait, we need to change the way we do business, you said they are being pulled out of your class too much, and you said we're not seeing the growth in scores, and you said"—I immediately jumped up and did a Multi-Flow Map. In the heated conversation, I was pulling in what everyone was saying and bringing it to the map, including all their ideas. In the moment, I grabbed a marker. It was the first time I understood objectifying emotions and being a third party in the room.*

The marker and the ensuing map Lynn created to represent the range of emotions from the participants was, in fact, a skillful use of the strategy of *externalization*. So often we will say to each other, "I see what you mean," but this is often a metaphorical placeholder for truly seeing and genuinely appreciating the wealth and expansiveness of another person's patterns of thinking. We often see our own version of another person's point of view from within our own frame of reference. With Thinking Maps, participants in the struggle to both *know what they mean* and *show what they know* have a visual language for representing their *internal*, complex, and nonlinear patterns of thinking *externally*. The focus shifts from the people involved to the ideas they discuss. As Lynn observed, her use of the maps sent an important signal to the individuals involved and the group as a whole: "I'm recognizing your concerns and including them as a cause in a box—what I hear you say is this." She concluded, "Putting it [their ideas] in a box, they all felt heard."

Next, Lynn shifted the discussion from the upset that people expressed to the goals they wanted for the gifted math services. Again, she turned to a Multi-Flow Map, which the group could use to identify the outcomes they hoped the implementation of the gifted math services would achieve. She noted, "So we went to the right side of the Multi-Flow Map and listed what we wanted to achieve—improved math thinking, increased scores, et cetera. Then, we went to a Tree Map to identify funding sources." As Lynn explained, members of the faculty got lost in the emotional content of the discussion, losing sight of what they had intended to accomplish and the purpose of the changes they had instituted. The maps, she observed, took "the emotion out of it so we could go back and see what we said we wanted and needed, why are we changing and what we problem solved. This put the data on the board." Making the data evident enabled them to see that the pull-out program affected the students' achievement. Lynn noted:

> *It got it out of the personal. This is what I like most about using the maps in leadership. Once you start solving emotional problems in the moment, it is amazing what it does. It is the only tool I know that works so simply like that. Democracy is not time efficient—yet this is a tool that makes it possible.*

Lynn shared that on a survey of working conditions conducted by the North Carolina Department of Public Instruction, teachers at Yates Mill reported feeling more empowered. She noted, "Thinking Maps give us a structure so that we are problem solving together. With the maps, the learner owns the learning, and as a leader I'm empowering people to make decisions and to *see* how it all makes sense." Thinking Maps enable the faculty to document the *why* or the journey of an entire meeting discussion and then use those visual representations to analyze what should be done. Lynn commented how, before using Thinking Maps at meetings in this way, someone would have just taken notes. "It would have just been auditory," she observed. "But now, we all walk away with an understanding."

The Well of Emotions

The insights from Lynn and her staff and from the Vertical Team at Blackham School came through *clarity* and *efficiency* and *collaboration* of the most difficult and often conflicted kind, leading thinkers across a school not only to feel *empowered*, but also to better know the power of their own minds. This also means they can stay in heated discussions and staff meetings that might otherwise go awry and *sustain* a conversation about hard data without driving down into what often feels like a bottomless well of emotions or a competition of ideas. Gradually, confidence (and trust) in self, the group, and the organization as a whole develops and helps create a culture of sustainability over the years.

In the course of human interactions, issues easily become quite complex and murky as emotions inform and influence them. Often people feel challenged to remain dispassionate in these interactions, believing that they must set aside their emotions in order to see and think clearly. Attempts to suppress emotions can, however, have the opposite effect on achieving clarity as emotions can be powerful and useful forces in guiding and informing thinking.

However, unconsciously allowing emotions to direct thinking and actions can also lead to what some refer to as an *emotional hijack* in which emotional filters not only inform but control our actions. Daniel Goleman et al. (2002) write, "The prefrontal area [of the brain] can veto an emotional impulse. . . . Without that veto, the result would be an emotional hijack, where the amygdala's impulse is acted upon" (p. 29). Such impulsive actions are often taken defensively and aggressively (fight-or-flight) and can cause irreparable harm in already delicate relationships. Power and authority often expressed in hierarchically defined and exercised roles also contribute to situations in which emotions can easily create misunderstandings and misguided and unproductive actions.

Many of our respondents viewed Thinking Maps as the visual and practical extension of the brain's executive functioning. From the routine task of designing and executing a simple plan to the more demanding challenge of responding to the endless stream of information and the intricacies of human dynamics in the workplace, each person worked overtime to lead in a positive, constructive, and sometimes visionary direction. Thinking Maps, as we have seen and heard, were indispensable in building, supporting, and enhancing the capacity of the brain to activate memory and language, direct attention to achieve both short- and long-term goals, and resolve issues of moral and ethical complexity, with emotions as a guide, not as the determinant. This highly attuned orchestration of thought and feeling results in what Goleman et al. (2002) call *resonant leadership,* or the ability to skillfully, respectfully, and effectively organize and inspire the feelings and thoughts of others as well as oneself toward shared goals.

The use of Thinking Maps helps remove artificial boundaries or separateness that narrow interpretations of role relationships can impose. The maps create a visual landscape that allows individuals to express and contextualize the holism of ideas through multiple thinking processes and frames of reference. The nature of this representation system—its grounding in inherent cognitive skills and intimate alignment with how the brain interacts with ideas and phenomena—sets it apart from other visual models or graphic organizers and allows it to function as a common visual language across roles as well as ages. The opportunity to fully represent the holism of their ideas clearly empowered many of those we interviewed. Former Superintendent Veronica McDermott observes, "Since the maps are rooted in the psychology of cognition, they, too, push users to be creative and to propel their thinking beyond the obvious."

The maps foster deeper attention to one's own thinking and to the ideas of others in a way that fundamentally changes the nature of the interaction. As one leader commented, "The maps are inevitably collaborative." They enable people to participate in the collective construction of meaning. In doing so, they support a type of listening that literally and figuratively *draws* users into the dialogue and enables them to attend deeply to what is expressed. This type of listening, what Art Costa (2008a) refers to in part as *generative listening,* occurs when "you can slow your mind's hearing to your ears' natural speed and hear beneath the words to their meaning" (p. 33). Just as Milton Glaser (2008) describes the act of drawing something as the opportunity to truly know it, literally drawing out ideas *draws* us to them, enabling us to take the time to listen and look deeply for the essence that exists beneath the surface.

For many interviewees, the use of Thinking Maps altered that internal dialogue and reframed their interactions with others in such a way as to allow for greater clarity and reciprocity. As Lambert (2009) asserts, "The brain's capacity to find patterns and make sense of the world is liberated within such relationships that encourage mutual care and equitable engagement" (p. 11). So often, people describe the experience of using Thinking Maps in group settings as literally finding themselves on the same page with others involved. This is not to say that agreement is automatically achieved. Rather, a space is opened in which all involved enter as equal partners in the generation of ideas as they work toward shared meanings and sound decisions. The purposeful, focused interaction that the use of Thinking Maps facilitates can be quite disarming in a positive sense. Thinking Maps suspend the impulse to compartmentalize things or arrive prematurely at clarity. Instead, drawing out their own and others' thinking allows people to become part of what Joseph Jaworski describes as *the unfolding* in which we accept others as "legitimate human beings" (Jaworski & Flowers, 1998, p. 11) and appreciate the ever-changing nature of our world and our constantly evolving understanding of it. In this way, we genuinely engage in the process of meaning making, an act of individual and collective construction that rejects the illusion of fixity and embraces the challenge and pleasure of living in a world of continual possibility.

Universal Themes of Connective Leadership

Because these themes of clarity, efficiency, collaboration, empowerment, and sustainability were so readily and uniformly identified and articulated, it might be concluded that they represent universal themes of central importance to people in leadership positions in school settings. However, it seems necessary to pause for a moment and ask whether these themes are vestiges of an antiquated model and reflect the habits of those who developed along with that system or, even so, whether they remain relevant in the current environment in which we live.

As Dickmann and Stanford-Blair (2002) propose in their book *Connecting Leadership to the Brain*, leadership, like all human behavior, evolves within an environmental context. Adapting to changes in the environment is necessary for all humans to survive and thrive, and the same holds true for those in leadership positions. They write, "The practice of leadership is not exempt from such contextual influence. Thus, the exercise of leadership in human culture responds to different contexts by making adjustments in the leadership behaviors engaged to influence others in goal achievement" (p. 126). While the endpoint remains the same—goal achievement—what adjustments in leadership behaviors are necessitated by the changes in the environmental conditions and human needs?

When asked what she looked for in the people she hired, Ursula Burns, the CEO of Xerox, answered, "I want them to be confident and uncertain" (as cited in Bryant, 2010). In a speech he delivered at a conference on international education, Michael Eskew, the CEO of UPS offered a similar statement regarding the qualities he valued in his workforce: "Learning how to learn is a trait we will always value" (Eskew, 2005, p. 5). What, then, do these two leaders of major corporations recognize about the current realities of the business environment that caused them to respond so similarly and, to some people, so unexpectedly? Both appear to recognize that a major condition of the current environment is change—and rapid change at that—and that agility as a learner will enable one to thrive and continue to contribute to the organization regardless of the changes that occur.

What implications, then, does this new environment have for leadership practices in which there can be no *illusion of fixity*, not out of despair but with great optimism? Dickmann and Stanford-Blair (2002) suggest, "It is the leader who acts mindfully, nurturing her or his own intelligence and the intelligence of others, who sets the tone for an organization poised to be successful in the new century" (p. 133).

So it would seem that clarity, efficiency, collaboration, empowerment, and sustainability remain relevant as important aspirations for leaders in their practice insofar as these are not only connected to their own individual purposes but enhance the capacity of others within the organization to achieve these levels in their work as well.

In the next chapter, we will hear the story of an entire school system that believed the fulfillment of its obligation to prepare its students for success in the 21st century depended on its becoming a thinking system. However, as Dickmann and Stanford-Blair (2002) point out, "Meaningful change or progress occurs only when what is envisioned is translated into specific action" (p. 55). That's where Thinking Maps come in.

Systems Thinking

"If we're not teaching *thinking*, then what are we doing?" With those words, Donna DeSiato, superintendent of East Syracuse Minoa Central School District in central New York, guided the transformation of her system.

Donna and her colleagues decided to address the issue of underachievement in their schools. They wanted to determine how best to change this pattern of low performance to intentionally teach about and for cognitive development. Rather than simply look to increase test scores through this effort, however, they chose to address the larger, more important question, How do we best prepare our youth for a complex, interconnected, changing world?

They believed the answer to this question would not only result in increased achievement but fulfill a much more important obligation they felt they had to their students. Summarizing the conversations within the leadership team, Donna DeSiato and Judy Morgan, the executive director of curriculum, instruction, and accountability, wrote:

> *We reasoned that our students were now facing an ever-increasing content knowledge base through a range of technologies and a future that envisions the need for people in college and the workforce to be highly adaptive, collaborative, self-reflective, creative and analytic thinkers. (DeSiato & Morgan, in press, p. 1)*

Before concluding our case studies with a complete description of the impact of Thinking Maps on the entire East Syracuse Minoa system under Donna's leadership, let's examine more broadly how *thinking* in *maps* fits into the complex dynamics of *leading change* in schools and systems. Defining the context and frame of reference at this point in our history—the early stage of the 21st century—is essential for understanding how Thinking Maps as a language for learning and leading fit into the picture.

Painting the Big Picture

The big picture in the wider field of education today is being painted with big ideas, especially in linking leading and learning to the dynamic workplace of a global economy, what many refer to as 21st century skills. Strangely, so many theorists and critics turn to the business world for answers about leadership. Only rarely do they look to breakthroughs from within the educational community itself. As Michael Fullan (1999) directly expresses in citing the eight forces of change or lessons as he refers to them, the process of change is complex and ambiguous. He summarizes the lessons as follows (p. 18):

Lesson 1: Moral Purpose Is Complex and Problematic

Lesson 2: Theories of Change and Theories of Education Need Each Other

Lesson 3: Conflict and Diversity Are Our Friends

Lesson 4: Understand the Meaning of Operating on the Edge of Chaos

Lesson 5: Emotional Intelligence Is Anxiety Provoking and Anxiety Containing

Lesson 6: Collaborative Cultures Are Anxiety Provoking and Anxiety Containing

Lesson 7: Attack Incoherence: Connectedness and Knowledge Creation Are Critical

Lesson 8: There Is No Single Solution: Craft Your Own Theories and Actions by Being a Critical Consumer

As noted earlier, this is what Marcie Roberts, director of Norman Howard School, was up against: her board had a positive working relationship; board members even had the visioning process down and a strategic plan in hand. However, it was complex and comprehensive, ambiguous, and ultimately unwieldy for people stretched by time. This also occurred for Mr. K's students, who worked each day across at least five subject areas with five different teachers—not only attempting to master the content, but also trying to understand the concepts that were the actual structure of the content.

Educational theorists, practitioners, researchers, parents, businesspeople, politicians, and social visionaries all grasp for conceptual definitions of leadership, learning, and even school in this flat, virtual world (Friedman, 2005). Relatively new fields—brain research in the neurosciences and new technologies—drive the conversation into uncharted territory and challenge educators to rethink what education is in a networked landscape. Scanning this landscape, educators may become overwhelmed by both the complexity of the problem and the wide array of solutions. Surely, one of the turning-point texts in the field of change dynamics and organizational learning came in 1990 when Peter Senge (1990b) and his colleagues described guiding disciplines for learning organizations: personal mastery, mental models, shared vision, team learning, and systems thinking. Educators and education leaders were caught in the embarrassing conundrum of being devoted to learning yet behind the curve as dynamic, cutting-edge learning organizations.

As *leading as learning* in schools becomes the catchphrase, many theorists and commentators attempt to mesh so many models of leading with an even wider array of definitions of learning. Yet a current runs through each and offers a focal point for uniting leading and learning. Howard Gardner (2006), who helped break open a new theory of multiple intelligences in the mid-1980s, offers, in *Five Minds for the Future*, the disciplined, synthesizing, creating, respectful, and ethical minds. In *A Whole New Mind*, author Daniel Pink (2006) projects a mind based on design, story, symphony, empathy, play, and meaningfulness. The implication from both Gardner and Pink is we need to focus education on the development of the mind. In turn, we should base leadership on the same paradigm shift. In the first decade of the 21st century, the blend between leadership and learning has become even more specific. Tony Wagner, codirector of the Change Leadership Group at the Harvard Graduate School of Education, links schools to the new world of work with 21st century survival skills. Wagner, a former teacher, school leader, and cofounder of Educators for Social Responsibility, interviewed corporate leaders and educators and, in stark terms, put his findings up against the antiquated focus of learning and the damaging educational testing practices that box up the mind (Wagner, 2008). He offers seven skill areas as a roadmap for transforming the larger goals of schools and leadership:

1. Critical thinking and problem solving

2. Collaboration across networks and leading by influence

3. Agility and adaptability

4. Initiative and entrepreneurialism

5. Effective oral and written communication

6. Accessing and analyzing information

7. Curiosity and imagination

Similarly, Linda Darling-Hammond (2010) proposes in her book *The Flat World and Education* that to succeed in the 21st century, students must have the capacity to design, evaluate, and manage their own work; frame, investigate, and solve problems using a wide range of tools; collaborate strategically with other people; communicate effectively in many forms; find, analyze, and use information for many purposes; and have the capacity to develop new products and ideas. Wagner and Darling-Hammond both set forth an enormous challenge for educational systems. The challenge, however, is not simply whether or not students have the capacity to develop these essential skills (of course they do). The challenge largely rests with whether or not teachers and school leaders are capable enough to teach these skills. The answer to this question will not ultimately depend on their understanding of and appreciation for the significance of these skills and the implications for curriculum and pedagogy. It will depend instead on whether or not those working in the field of education can embody these very same skills in their professional practice.

Senge (1990a, 1990b), Gardner (2006), Pink (2006), Wagner (2008), and many others richly illustrate the big-picture problem within the highly structured school walls in stark contrast to the messy and dynamic processes of the workplace. (It's important to note that Wagner looks only at innovative, successful companies, not those in bankruptcy or under compromised leadership. Also, we need to accept educational critics' assumption that we should replicate in our schools what we see in the global marketplace and in society at large.) Generally, if one believes in what these authors bring forward, then the key questions become:

How do we translate these big ideas about how the forest should be sustained into the practice of nurturing the individual trees? What is the bridge between where we are and where we want to be in schools, given their existing, nearly century-old structure? Of particular concern in this book is the direct link between leadership and teaching and learning practices in the 21st century school.

Take a bird's eye view of these grand theories, and you begin to realize a common thread that these authors all string together: the focus of education should be on *explicitly developing minds*—creative, analytic, reflective, and collaborative minds that consciously lead and learn with empathy, integrity, and symphony as global citizens of the 21st century. Let's dig down to the roots: while we want to engage the whole mind, where is the grounding? A very unlikely source for a synthesis of these works comes from David Brooks, a conservative columnist for the *New York Times*. In a May 2008 *New York Times* article, Brooks finds the root of the system in a column titled "The Cognitive Age." He writes in bold, unromantic terms about global competitiveness for individuals and the people who lead organizations:

> *The globalization paradigm emphasizes the fact that information can now travel 15,000 miles in an instant. But the most important part of information's journey is the last few inches—the space between a person's eyes or ears and the various regions of the brain. Does the individual have the capacity to understand the information? Does he or she have the training to exploit it? Are there cultural assumptions that distort the way it is perceived? (Brooks, 2008)*

Whereas Senge (1990a, 1990b), Gardner (2006), Pink (2006), Wagner (2008), and other researchers and practitioners may rightly perceive this view as highly reductionist and lacking moral vision, Brooks states the obvious: it is no longer the information age, the age of technology, or even some sort of high-minded age of reason for the elite in our society. It is everyone's cognitive age. As educators, we contain within our dry and often forgotten mission statements the intellectual or *cognitive* development of all children. We have only partially failed by seeing cognitive development faintly through a focus almost exclusively on content learning and, only until recently, mostly for a chosen few. This is an antiquated view. For all members of the school community, we now must match the vision of developing the whole mind—the minds of the next generation—as the core of the educational process in the 21st century with a theory-rich model for the systematic development of thinking for learning, teaching, and leading. If we don't see this vision of thinking as a foundation for leadership, we will never see this as the foundation for learning.

Teaching, Leading, and Learning in an Interconnected World

The East Syracuse Minoa Central School District comprises a preschool for three- to four-year-olds, four elementary schools, a middle school, and a high school with a total district enrollment of approximately 3,800 students. Covering seventy-two square miles, this suburban district had a six-year trend of fairly midrange scores in English language arts and math. While not alarming, a close look at the trend indicates that a significant gap existed between the abilities of district students and their performance.

Superintendent Donna DeSiato and her colleagues recognized that improvement in test scores alone would not sufficiently meet this challenge. They chose to undertake a much more comprehensive analysis of the current research in the field and its implications for their entire approach to teaching, leading, and learning. It would not be a simple tweaking of the system, Donna said as she reflected on the experience. Successfully meeting this challenge required, she and her team believed, a transformation at all levels.

> *Most often the focus of strategic planning is to strengthen or modify what currently exists and, indeed, we certainly believe in continuous improvement. However, in order to embrace the challenges, changes and opportunities of the 21st century, we discovered we needed to go beyond our existing system and our current paradigms which led us to the exploration of what many in the field are now calling 21st century skills. (DeSiato & Morgan, in press, p. 4)*

To begin this process, Donna and her colleagues clarified and redefined their goals, focusing on student learning and achievement and strategies for measuring the results. Because of their desire to challenge the assumptions on which their current system was built, East Syracuse Minoa began by revisiting its mission statement to be sure it reflected current realities and the educational direction the district wanted to move toward. Donna and her colleagues started this process with a series of questions, using a Tree Map (figure 7.1, page 114) to provide a shared visual landscape for generating these ideas together.

The mission statement identifies the following goals.

- **Goal 1:** Increase student achievement through high expectations supported by consistent, comprehensive focus on teaching and learning.

- **Goal 2:** Increase student achievement by building capacity within the system to support and nurture a continuum of learning through the implementation of research-based practices.

- **Goal 3:** Increase student achievement by strengthening parent engagement and community partnerships to support learning.

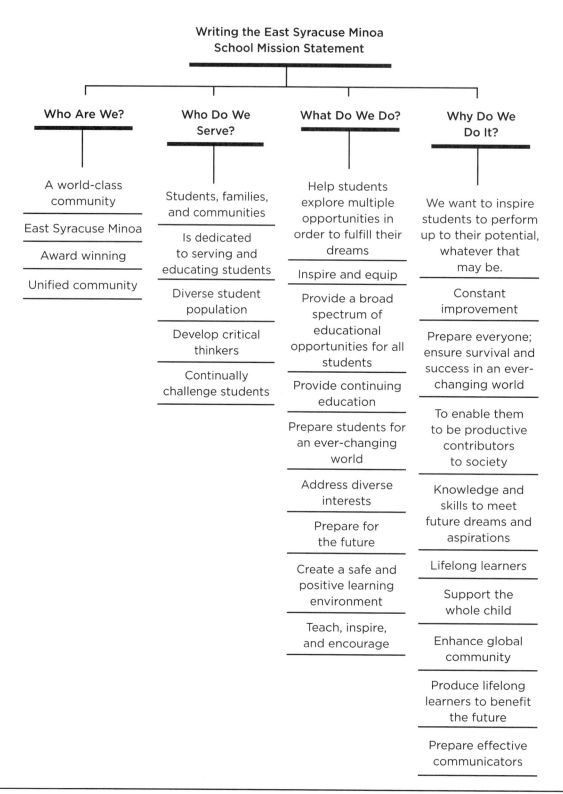

Figure 7.1: Sample Tree Map to generate the school's mission statement.

Donna and her colleagues understood that to be effective, the changes to their practices needed to be made systemically and required ongoing monitoring and assessment. They agreed to ultimately choose practices that aligned with their goals and resulted in improvement both on standardized tests and on measures that assessed the development of higher-order thinking skills.

Using Research-Informed Decision Making

To begin this process, each of the seven schools in the East Syracuse Minoa district formed an improvement team. Each team included representation from teachers, instructional staff, parents, and administrators. A common charge to all was to engage in a thorough review of the current research in the field on effective practices. The work of Marzano et al. (2001) provided a common framework at the time from which to conduct an investigation into those practices that held the greatest promise for improving student learning. One of the most effective instructional practices that Marzano et al. identified in their meta-analysis of the research on effective teaching was the use of nonlinguistic representation. Additionally, their work highlighted the ability of students to identify similarities and differences in ideas and concepts, meaningfully summarize and take notes, generate and test hypotheses, and work cooperatively with others as critical to successful learning. The development of these abilities supported by teaching practices that provided high-quality feedback, employed higher-order questioning, and used advanced cues and organizers to prepare students for deep engagement in new content and experiences would result in improved student learning and achievement.

As the teams expanded their investigation to identify specific approaches that might address these areas, they concluded that Thinking Maps represented a unique opportunity to unite students across all grade levels and in all content areas through the use of a common visual language for thinking. Because Thinking Maps were not content- or grade-level specific, and because they were specifically designed to promote and strengthen the skillful use of fundamental cognitive processes for all learning, the improvement teams felt Thinking Maps were ideally suited for the systemic approach to improving student learning they believed was essential to changing the pattern of underachievement in their district.

Donna and her colleagues reported impressive results as all teachers used the maps and introduced them to students within the first three years of implementation. A team of administrators and instructional leaders became certified as Thinking Maps trainers through an intensive program. Subsequently, they provided the professional development to their teaching colleagues that included the initial introduction of Thinking Maps and systematic follow-up support during the first three years of the implementation. With the internal expertise in place, East Syracuse Minoa had the capacity to ensure that any teacher new to the system would be introduced to the work with Thinking Maps and thus be provided with an uninterrupted, continuous experience for the students. For those teachers already in the system, expertise was immediately available to support their continued effort to integrate these tools into their teaching practices.

The research findings of Marzano et al. (2001) on which the improvement teams had based the decision to implement Thinking Maps proved to be true in their own experience. As Donna noted, "We observed the transformation of our system as the maps were introduced to all teachers at all grade levels within the first three years of implementation." She went on to add, "During the second and third year we witnessed the powerful and positive impact of building upon prior learning as students progressed from one grade to the next and from one area of content to another." Rather than having isolated and episodic experiences, students had the opportunity over time to develop their fluency with integrating and applying the eight Thinking Maps and the Frame of Reference to facilitate their thinking, their understanding of content and concepts, and ultimately their success in learning.

The engagement of representatives from all aspects of the school community in this process and their sustained commitment to the implementation helped produce the outcomes they believed were possible. In a letter written to the principal of each East Syracuse Minoa school, New York State Commissioner of Education Richard Mills states, "You and your entire school community are to be commended for leading New York forward to accomplish our dual goals of increasing student achievement while closing the gap in student performance" (as cited in DeSiato & Morgan, in press, p. 4).

For many schools, achievement of this dimension would have been cause for celebration, and the task would have been labeled *accomplished*. For Donna and her colleagues, however, while they celebrated their success, it represented only the beginning.

Becoming a Thinking School System in the 21st Century

"We learn through the process of composing questions," Executive Director of Curriculum, Instruction, and Accountability, Judy Morgan, observed. Furthermore, we not only learn through this process but lead that way as well. In the process of working with Thinking Maps, the use of questions and an inquiry approach to learning was constantly reinforced throughout the system. During the implementation of Thinking Maps, the East Syracuse Minoa district continued its exploration of 21st century learning. Naturally, then, teachers looked more deeply at the results they had achieved and questioned the degree to which these results reflected their larger goal of preparing students for a rapidly changing world. Rather than simply accept the data as fact, they chose to ask questions they might not normally ask— questions that would challenge them to not simply look for affirmation of what they hoped to achieve but to genuinely probe the data to see what they truly revealed about their efforts.

Suspecting they might have only strengthened learning in the content areas, a result that was significant but fell short of their ultimate goal, they posed the following questions: What is the relationship between thinking and learning? What does thinking look like in our classrooms? These questions compelled East Syracuse Minoa to re-examine how Thinking Maps were being implemented, and they stimulated a burst of activity in which teachers explored and expanded their efforts to improve both student learning and student thinking using these same tools. However, even this flurry of activity and the proceeding positive results fell short of one of the major ideas that framed the district's approach to transforming its entire system for 21st century learning. From the beginning, teachers had committed to not simply *tweaking* the system but transforming it at all levels. Once again the answer came in the form of questions. They asked themselves, "What do all leaders in our system need to be successful in *leading* so that our district can be successful in learning with all students?" "What is the relationship between leading, learning, and thinking throughout all levels of the organization, and how do we support and develop that relationship systemically?"

As a learning community, East Syracuse Minoa was committed to pursuing clarity through collaborative processes that engaged people throughout the system's educational community, including parents and community members. Generating the level of commitment needed to make and sustain the changes the district sought to achieve required not just the participation of people but the skillful participation that Lambert (2007) describes. The leadership in East Syracuse Minoa recognized that to welcome people to become actively involved or even to distribute to them various leadership responsibilities was not enough. As well intended as these actions might be, the potential existed that people would become frustrated and disillusioned by the experience or, worse, feel set up and betrayed. Providing people with tools and strategies to guide the process and not simply be guided by it, however, would genuinely empower school community members to assert themselves as leaders. As a common visual language for learning and leading, Thinking Maps represented an ideal opportunity to bring coherence to this change effort and unite all members of the educational community. The culture of inquiry the district sought to promote and sustain in its classrooms and throughout its entire organization could be supported by the youngest to the oldest members of the educational community speaking the same language.

Leading Thinkers

As the work with Thinking Maps in the classrooms made advances in student learning and achievement, East Syracuse Minoa started to experience staffing changes due to retirement and other reasons. Thus, the district added another question to the ones previously stated, How can we strengthen the system to withstand these naturally occurring changes? Donna and her colleagues recognized that addressing this reality was not simply a matter of succession planning—identifying who would step into specific roles as they became vacated. It was again a systemic challenge that involved not only deciding who would serve as leaders within the system but how to equip those leaders and the system, in general, to function collectively and cohesively at the highest levels of performance.

In the 21st century, information is generated and travels at such rapid rates, and the need for people to individually and collectively assimilate and network that information intelligently and to transform it into purposeful, actionable knowledge is critical to the success of any school's mission. East Syracuse Minoa challenged itself to develop Shirley Hord's (1997) characterization of such a systemic dynamic as communities of continuous inquiry and improvement. This idea of ongoing organizational growth and development depended on leadership designed to promote and thrive in an environment of purposeful dialogue, innovation, and meaningful engagement at all levels of the school community. In such settings in fact, opportunities for leadership are seen as constantly emerging. It becomes the expectation and even the culture of the system in general that regardless of any formal designation, all members of the school community will assert themselves and their ideas in collaborative processes to improve learning for all with the educational community. Only through such individual and collective effort and efficacy did East Syracuse Minoa believe it could sustain its improvement efforts and withstand changes beyond its immediate control.

"First and foremost," Donna stated, "we knew that all of our leaders needed knowledge of effective research-based practices and an understanding of how to implement these practices systemically." East Syracuse Minoa leaders recognized that Thinking Maps presented a unique opportunity for people within the system to develop a deeper understanding of this work through their own use of the maps for various leadership purposes. "As we focused on realigning and strengthening our learning organization," note DeSiato and Morgan, "we discovered that we had the tools needed to enhance, facilitate and assess critical thinking, problem-solving, collaborating and communicating in Thinking Maps" (DeSiato & Morgan, in press, p. 7). As a descriptive language and as visual patterns for generating, organizing, and communicating thinking, the district saw the maps as the ideal complement to its effort to transform learning at all levels of the school community.

With the goal of enhancing critical thinking, problem solving, and communication throughout their learning organization, members of the core leadership team at East Syracuse Minoa participated in an intensive two-day Thinking Maps leadership training at their summer institute. Commenting on this decision, Deputy Superintendent, Thomas Neveldine, observed:

> ESM made a commitment to implement Thinking Maps through extensive professional development and support for practice at all levels of the system. The uses of Thinking Maps are invaluable in working with a variety of school personnel and community groups to produce meaningful outcomes. The process has an understandable logic and provides a roadmap for engaging participants in dialogue around critical issues, providing a visual representation of their thinking. (as cited in DeSiato & Morgan, in press, p. 8)

Shifting the Question

A typical approach to inviting people into the process of exchanging ideas and collaborative problem solving is to ask them what they think. Intended to increase participation and representation of multiple points of view, leading with this question often results in something quite different. Without the opportunity to surface thoughts individually or create a shared understanding of the topic or challenge, some people feel compelled to stake out a territory with a thought. Other participants in the meeting might withdraw in silence and wait to hear what others say as they try to formulate their own ideas. It is not unusual for such interactions to devolve into a competition of ideas, with some people finding it necessary to defend a position they took prematurely. Others, including those who have put forward an idea and those waiting to do so, might listen only for affirmation of their own thinking, looking to strengthen their position and thus sacrificing greater possibilities to their own certainty. This competition of ideas rarely results in outcomes that have the genuine support and enthusiasm of the collective body, nor does it have the advantages of a true dialogue in bringing to the surface the fullest expression of the possible ideas. Complex issues are potentially reduced to battles of ideologies and conceits that individual agendas frequently distort.

At East Syracuse Minoa, as in other districts using Thinking Maps for leadership practices, a fundamental shift in the quality of the discourse occurred when the process began with the question, How do we want to think about this? As Donna and Judy observed, this approach interrupted the impulse to assume clarity and instead created the conditions for genuine inquiry. From the question, What thinking do we need to solve this problem, to deepen our collective understanding, to develop shared understanding, and to create new knowledge?, a process of inquiry could unfold with all participants able to enter it as learners with the potential to develop both individual and collective insight.

The significance of this shift underscored a profound realization on the part of the leadership team in East Syracuse Minoa. These leaders recognized the need for alignment in the actions of the adults in the system with the beliefs they espoused and subscribed to in order for their students to succeed as adults in the 21st century. As DeSiato and Morgan state:

> Importantly, for the adult learners in our school system and wider learning community, the processes and approaches we use must carry some degree of transferability into our day-to-day lives. If not, then how can we say in authentic terms that we are giving students tools that can be used outside of the classroom? We have found that Thinking Maps are useful tools, not just in schools, but in our daily lives. We, as citizens of our world, have a responsibility to make decisions that are thoughtful and demonstrate responsibility for ourselves and others. (DeSiato & Morgan, in press, p. 10)

Walking the Talk

The unfortunate reality in most school systems is that very little time is available to think about, plan, and discuss the actions necessary to improve the educational outcomes. Most people who need to participate in these essential processes are engaged in teaching or leading during the workday. Opportunities for meaningful engagement are rare or episodic and often occur at additional expense to the system or in sacrifice of contact time with students. The work life of teachers and school leaders is structured around the day-to-day requirements of the job—the lessons to be taught, the meetings to be held, the crisis to be solved, and so on. Some people liken the process of school change efforts by those within the system to trying to fix a moving car.

It is not surprising, then, in this context that efficiency would continually emerge in our research as a significant benefit people derive from using Thinking Maps for leadership practices. As one East Syracuse Minoa assistant principal noted, "We have very limited time for committee work, and Thinking Maps help us more efficiently to get the information we need to get at." Several of the school leaders in East Syracuse Minoa referenced this tangible by-product of the work done in committees. With the use of Thinking Maps, they saw meetings as being more productive and having greater continuity from one to the next. They noted that assignments and responsibilities between meetings were also explicit and resulted in greater accountability and efficiency. In particular, they identified the central importance of formulating questions to guide the selection of the Thinking Maps critical to their effectiveness as leaders. As leaders of learning in these settings, their use of Thinking Maps strengthened the use of inquiry-based processes and supported people's participation and engagement. Because all committee members were familiar with the language of Thinking Maps, no one member had greater influence over the others in their use. Participants in the meetings could literally and figuratively be on the same page and speaking the same language as they drew out the emerging patterns of thinking and engaged in constructive dialogue.

An example of this occurred with the high school guidance department in a meeting that the principal and executive director of curriculum, instruction, and accountability led. They needed to address significant problems within the department, and previous attempts to do so ended in raised voices and finger-pointing. The fact that there had been seven principals in four years certainly contributed to the lack of coordination and effectiveness this department demonstrated. The principal worried this meeting might repeat the pattern of miscommunication and be unproductive or, worse, counterproductive by furthering the tension that already existed within the department. He sought the involvement of the executive director who had more experience with Thinking Maps, and together they developed a process for the meeting. Naturally, they decided to begin the meeting with asking a question—"What would a highly effective guidance department look like?"

They chose a Circle Map (figure 7.2) to initiate the process of defining a go-to guidance department. As past history might predict, there was silence at first as people were reluctant to speak, cautious in their approach with each other. In situations in which the exchange of ideas is purely verbal and there is an underlying tension, dialogue is often inhibited, and defensive postures are assumed. The introduction of a Thinking Map, the Circle Map, provided a safe and common ground for participants in this meeting to focus their attention and begin to contribute their ideas.

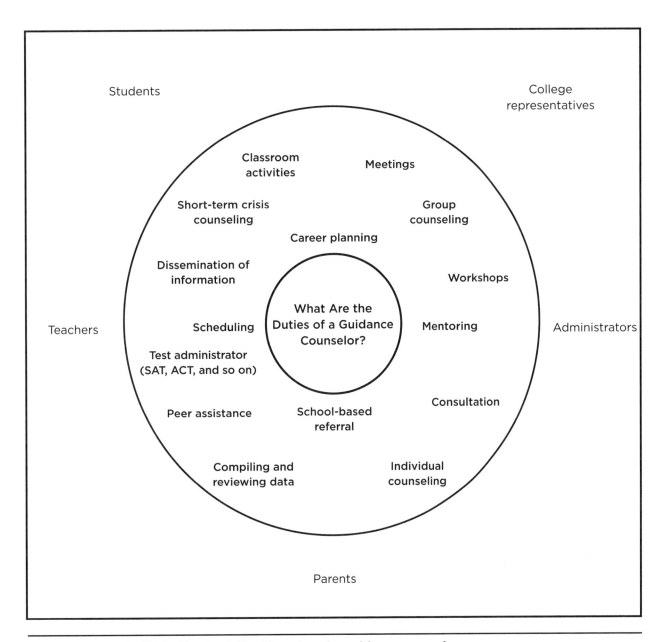

Figure 7.2: Sample Circle Map to define the roles of a guidance counselor.

As the group members generated ideas, they began to identify patterns and acknowledge missing things—certain procedures and systems, for example, that would improve their effectiveness as a department. Facilitators did not prompt this exchange, but it arose naturally as the participants responded to the display of ideas. Adding a new source to their Frame of Reference, the coordinator shared some information about the national recommendations for areas in which guidance counselors should spend time and approximately what percent of time they should spend in those areas. The group decided on its own to create a Tree Map (figure 7.3, page 122) with these areas and organize the information from its Circle Map under these categories.

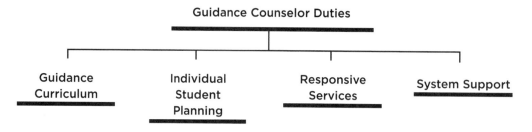

Figure 7.3: Sample Tree Map to further define the roles of a guidance counselor.

As a next step, the group members decided to estimate the percentage of time they actually spent on the different areas and use that information to make adjustments, as necessary, in their allocation of time and resources. The meeting ended at that point because of time, but as the executive director observed and the principal concurred, "It was a very energizing meeting, with everyone participating, and no one left angry or frustrated." The principal immediately began to plan for the next meeting hoping to build on the momentum this experience produced. The use of the maps had a visible and tangible effect on the climate and productivity of the meeting. Reflecting on this, the executive director noted, "I just continue to be amazed at the opportunities that the maps provide for us to grow as a system."

In this brief but no less significant example, the use of Thinking Maps supported all of the major themes we have identified and that surfaced in our research. As the principal and the executive director noted, they conducted the meeting efficiently, and the group achieved clarity on the topic with relative ease. Perhaps most significantly, the shift in attention to the ideas and not the personalities that the use of the maps promoted improved the level of collaboration and empowered the group to direct the course of the interaction. As Diane Zimmerman, school superintendent and contributing author to *The Constructivist Leader*, observes, "When group members become excited about the emerging relevance of the conversation the group self-organizes around the emerging concepts" (1995, p. 105). This phenomenon was clearly evident in this meeting in which the members of the guidance department responded to the ideas being generated and became thoroughly immersed in the process. With growing confidence and assurance, they participated enthusiastically in the processes of reflection, inquiry, and dialogue—the very same processes that the school itself intended to promote for its students. They collectively decided on the direction their study of this topic needed to take and set the agenda for carrying it forward. Having gotten the group started with the use of the Circle Map, the executive director and the principal could move to the background and allow the group to assume responsibility for the completion of its work.

With Thinking Maps as tools for collaborative thinking and problem solving, members of this group will likely be able to sustain their constructive engagement with each other beyond this meeting and, with growing confidence in themselves, transfer this experience to other settings. The influence of this experience on the principal was equally significant. By asking for and receiving support from a colleague for this meeting and experiencing a successful outcome as a result, the principal became more intent on using the maps proactively in his leadership practice. Increasingly, the use of Thinking Maps both shaped and reinforced the culture of East Syracuse Minoa as a thinking school system.

Connecting Multiple Voices, Multiple Minds for a Common Purpose

The strategic planning process East Syracuse Minoa undertook involved about eight hundred people. Eight hundred! To include that many people was quite ambitious, but district leaders were committed to reaching the full range of stakeholders in their community. Through focus forums, electronic and paper surveys, and a major event using the World Café process, members of the East Syracuse Minoa leadership team engaged the community in considering a series of key questions that were central to helping them decide the future direction of their system (East Syracuse Minoa Central School District, 2009).

- What skills and strategies will students need in order to be successful in our changing world?

- What are some of the practices and learning opportunities currently in place that promote student success?

- In order for our students to be successful in the future, how must East Syracuse Minoa's educational system shift?

- What is currently in place that will no longer prepare our students for the world as it shifts?

- What untapped resources does our community have to offer?

The district chose the World Café process because of its alignment with major goals of the system—representation from all aspects of the community and collaboration. The World Café process creates a living network of collaborative dialogue that mirrors the virtual world of the 21st century in which we exchange so much of our information. For this World Café process, the East Syracuse Minoa leadership team recruited people by reaching out to various community groups and organizations. Team members used Thinking Maps extensively throughout the process, but first to identify what they wanted to accomplish with this process in general (figure 7.4, page 124).

With such a diverse group, having a common language and a visual reference point for people to see and appreciate the richness of thinking was extremely helpful. As the process unfolded, the group began to build the common ground that would inform future processes and decisions.

The massive amount of information generated through the surveys, focus groups, and World Café process could have resulted in information overload. Here again, the group used

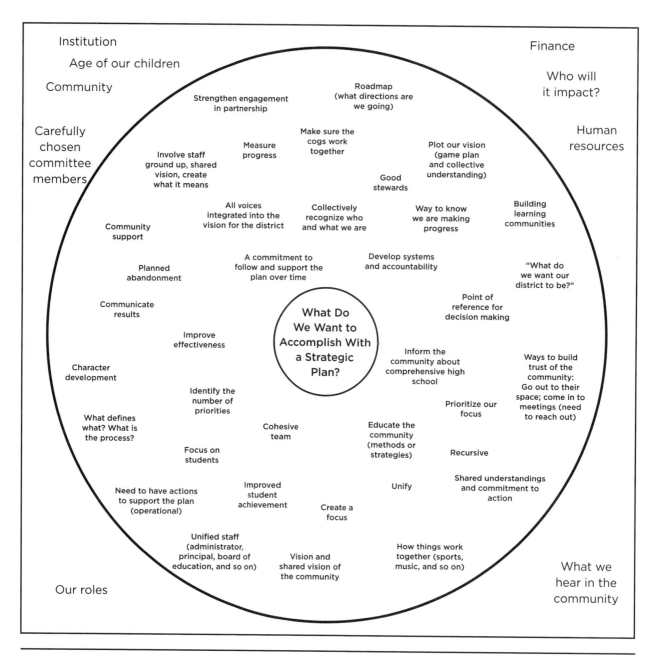

Figure 7.4: Sample Circle Map to identify what to accomplish with the strategic plan.

Thinking Maps effectively to generate, reflect on, and organize the information by identifying patterns and connections. As Judy described the process, "We literally made a Tree Map by sorting these topics into piles and then created five areas of focus." (See figure 7.5.)

This inductive process promoted further dialogue and clarification of the ideas the group generated. Starting with the Tree Map would have allowed for a greater emphasis on fitting the thinking to the categories rather than having the categories emerge through the natural connections that the group observed.

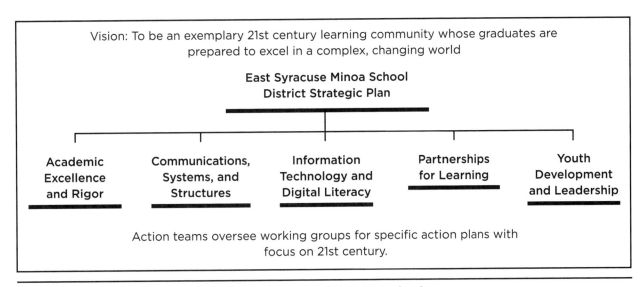

Figure 7.5: Sample Tree Map of the five main areas of the strategic plan.

Despite the number of participants and the amount of information generated, the World Café process proceeded efficiently and resulted in a clearly articulated document—including Tree Maps and details of groups' plans—that, as Judy described, "drives what we do and how we do it." Subsequently, subcommittees were formed to carry the work forward in each of the five areas, with progress noted and additional goals added. Each action team invested itself deeply in the process of generating action steps in response to the goals established for its area. One of the teams, the Academic Excellence and Rigor Action Team, engaged in an intensive process to create a detailed strategic plan. As the examples from the team's Tree Map show (figure 7.6, page 126), the plan included specific actions to address the overall goals, stated in measurable terms.

The emphasis was clearly on action. The use of the Tree Map made this evident and easily accessible to the entire school system community. Kathy Southwell, East Syracuse Minoa's director of teaching and learning, commented on the critical role the use of Thinking Maps played in the development of the action plan for this team and in communicating that information to others in a manner that did not overwhelm them.

In order to meet our district's vision, we are striving to effectively plan and implement significant educational change. As the facilitator of the Academic Excellence and Rigor Action Team and Subcommittees, I truly believe that the use of Thinking Maps has helped the synergy of ideas, created highly developed recommendations for change, and organized effective implementation plans. The Tree Map [figure 7.7, page 128] is the work of the Academic Excellence and Rigor Action Team in the second year of implementation of our strategic plan. Teachers, parents, and administrators were starting to feel overwhelmed by the magnitude of the different action items for this group, with questions being raised regarding the connection of some of this

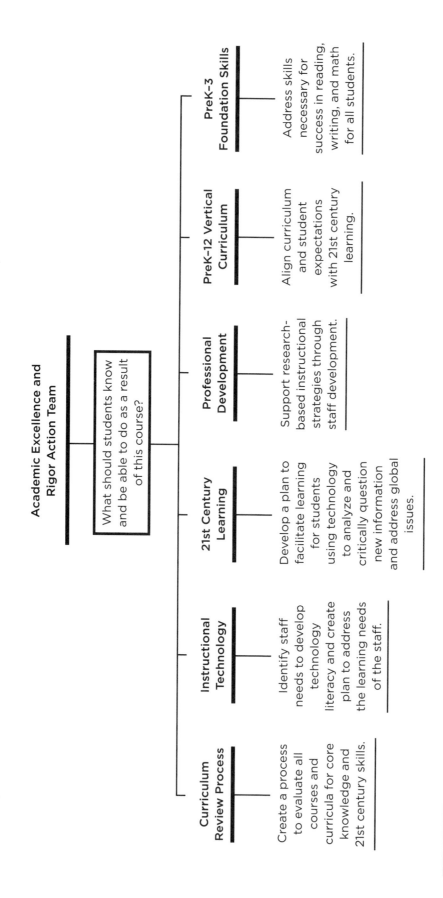

Academic Excellence and Rigor Action Team

What should students know and be able to do as a result of this course?

Curriculum Review Process

Create a process to evaluate all courses and curricula for core knowledge and 21st century skills.

Instructional Technology

Identify staff needs to develop technology literacy and create plan to address the learning needs of the staff.

21st Century Learning

Develop a plan to facilitate learning for students using technology to analyze and critically question new information and address global issues.

Professional Development

Support research-based instructional strategies through staff development.

PreK–12 Vertical Curriculum

Align curriculum and student expectations with 21st century learning.

PreK–3 Foundation Skills

Address skills necessary for success in reading, writing, and math for all students.

Figure 7.6: Sample Tree Map to address the goals of the strategic plan.

work with other ongoing initiatives in our district. This map was created to organize our thinking under the district's vision, show the connection with the five district strategic planning action teams, and make a connection with the DuFours' essential questions that have been widely used in our district to shape the work of our professional learning community. Once we established the structure at the top of the Tree Map, our discussion was rapidly focused and organized. (DeSiato & Morgan, in press, pp. 9–10)

Kathy's reflection captures the multiple benefits of using Thinking Maps in developing solutions to complex challenges by the maps' inherent ability to focus attention on the *thinking* necessary to make and implement such decisions. Carl Glickman (1993) proposes that "educators cannot teach students how to gain entry into the knowledge and power of the profound discussions of a democracy unless they themselves have gained entry into the knowledge and power of the profound discussions of their schools" (p. 28). The process that Kathy commented on—one that included representation from a range of stakeholders from the internal and external community of the school system—required a sophisticated approach in which the adult participants could grapple constructively and collaboratively with uncertainty and complexity. Thinking Maps provided participants in this process with entry points into the expression and appreciation for their own and each other's ideas. The visual nature of the maps allowed them to literally draw out their ideas, not in an idiosyncratic fashion, but in a way that all the participants immediately recognized. The Tree Map made the relationships between and among the information clearly evident. The conversations leading to the formulation of the categories surfaced new meanings and insights. Patterns could easily be discerned, and using the same language allowed all members of the action team to fully engage their individual and collective intelligence and creative potential.

Just as important, they fulfilled the challenge that Donna DeSiato and Judy Morgan had set for the adult community of the system to model the very practices and dispositions they believed students needed in order to succeed in the 21st century. Ken Kay, president of the Partnership for 21st Century Skills, stresses the importance of focusing on the four Cs: critical thinking and problem solving, communication, collaboration, and creativity and innovation (as cited in DeSiato & Morgan, in press). If the adults within the school community didn't strive to develop and demonstrate these same approaches in their own work, DeSiato and Morgan (in press) contend, "Then how can we say in authentic terms that we are giving students tools that can be used outside of the classroom?" (p. 10).

Forming a Community of Learners and Leaders

In addition to these meta-processes, the use of Thinking Maps began to permeate the culture of the East Syracuse Minoa educational system. Within the action teams and the time available for them to meet, they used Thinking Maps to help them efficiently address the topics in their portion of the strategic plan. Regardless of the action team a person served on, every

Academic Excellence and Rigor Action Team

Key initiative 1: We will identify core knowledge and establish curriculum that prioritizes essential learning that sets high expectations for all students.

1.1: To develop grade-level and content-area curriculum documents in standard format including essential questions, guiding questions, vocabulary, learning goals, required instructional strategies and resources, prior knowledge, and assessments

Kindergarten– through fifth-grade-level learning plan days were held in December 2008 to begin development of curriculum document for literacy in standard district format.

Sixth– through eighth-grade-level learning plan days were held February–March 2009 to begin development of curriculum document for literacy in standard district format.

1.2: To create a schedule to review and evaluate all curricula areas

Curriculum Review Processes subcommittee was formed in December 2008 with task of designing and recommending a curriculum review process for district to be implemented in 2009–2010. Subcommittee has representation from community, administration, and teachers.

January 2009 subcommittee researched and reviewed curriculum review process from other districts and began drafting the purpose statements for our curriculum review document.

March 2009 subcommittee meeting finalized purpose statement and began action steps.

1.5: To develop valid common assessments to guide instruction and monitor student learning

K–12 staff development days in October 2008 focused on common assessments and centered on difference between common formative and common summative assessments.

Teachers are using PLC time to develop and discuss common assessments.

Middle school and high school staff worked with national consultant Debra Pickering for two days in March 2009, focusing on grading practices and formative and summative assessments.

Figure 7.7: Excerpt from Academic Excellence and Rigor Action Team Tree Map.

member of the school community could easily communicate and understand the information from all teams through the common language of Thinking Maps. Without participating in the meetings, people could, without difficulty, reconstruct the conversations and trace the development of the thinking through the visual artifacts. Because each map displays the information through a particular thinking pattern, people's thinking and how they developed their ideas are evident to the viewer.

The Communications, Systems, and Structures Action Team created a Circle Map (figure 7.8) to generate ideas for improving communication between the school system and the community related to 21st century learning.

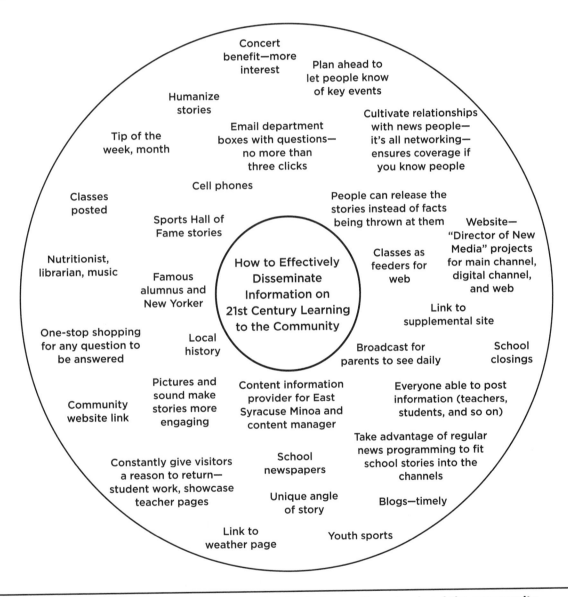

Figure 7.8: Sample Circle Map to improve communication between the school and the community.

Despite the extensive participation of people from throughout the community in the strategic planning process, the district wanted to ensure that links to the community remained active and people were continually updated and educated on the progress toward their goals. While not all the ideas included in the Circle Map would result in specific actions, the team would go on to use a Tree Map to group them and develop specific action steps to move forward on those of highest priority.

The Communications, Systems, and Structures Action Team chose to address the challenge of improving parent engagement at the elementary level as one of its goals. As a prelude to deciding how to actually improve parent engagement, this team began with the question, How will parent engagement in the future be similar to and different from the way it currently exists? Framing this discussion, of course, was the systemwide vision of East Syracuse Minoa becoming an "exemplary 21st century learning community whose graduates are prepared to excel in a complex, interconnected, changing world" (East Syracuse Minoa Central School District, n.d.). For this question, the team chose to begin with a Double Bubble Map (figure 7.9), a visual representation that would explicitly show the similarities and differences between the current state of parent engagement and the state of engagement the district desired to attain.

From this map, the group members would go on to decide how to strengthen and sustain those aspects of parental engagement they wanted to keep in place. They would also use the map as a starting point for deciding the action steps necessary to implementation of new approaches to achieving their vision for future parent engagement. Each time the question changed, they would use a different Thinking Map with a different cognitive lens to clarify the thinking and move the process forward.

Another group, the School to College and Career Advisory Board, began its work by asking the question, "What experiences should students be exposed to and required to do in order to promote career awareness, exploration, and decision making?" Again, the question was framed by East Syracuse Minoa's larger interest to prepare its students for 21st century living and learning. Not wanting to simply propose a number of interesting activities students could participate in, the team used the following question to ensure that the experiences it created supported the larger purpose, How will these experiences address the needs of the 21st century employer? The Circle Map (figure 7.10, page 132) represents the initial ideas the group generated, keeping in mind the needs of 21st century employers.

Coordination with the Academic Excellence and Rigor Action Team was an essential component of this process as the work of the two teams overlapped in significant ways. The use of the maps as a common way of representing the thinking of each team made it easy to access that information, see patterns, identify what might be missing, and ensure coherence throughout the system.

One elementary school principal described a process he developed for welcoming incoming kindergarten parents. Concerned that parents might negatively view his former experience

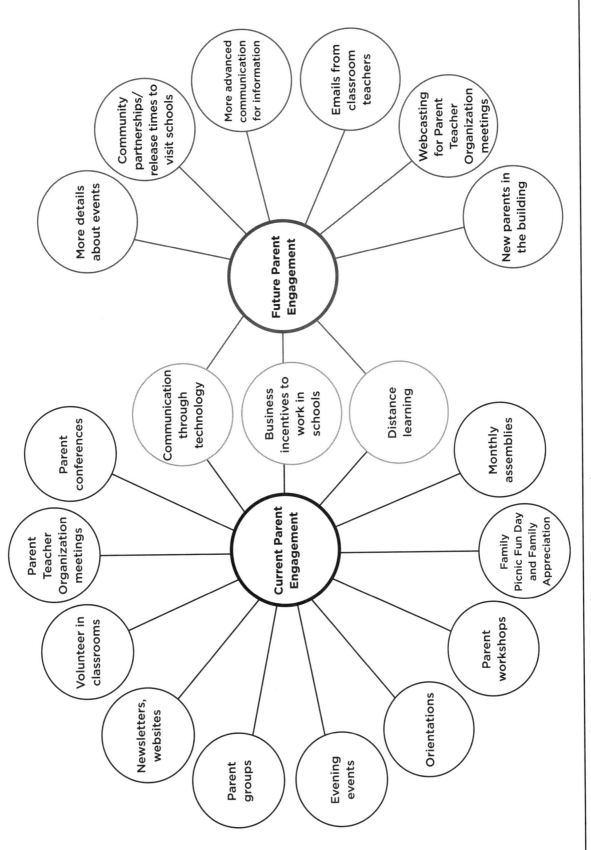

Figure 7.9: Sample Double Bubble Map of parent engagement.

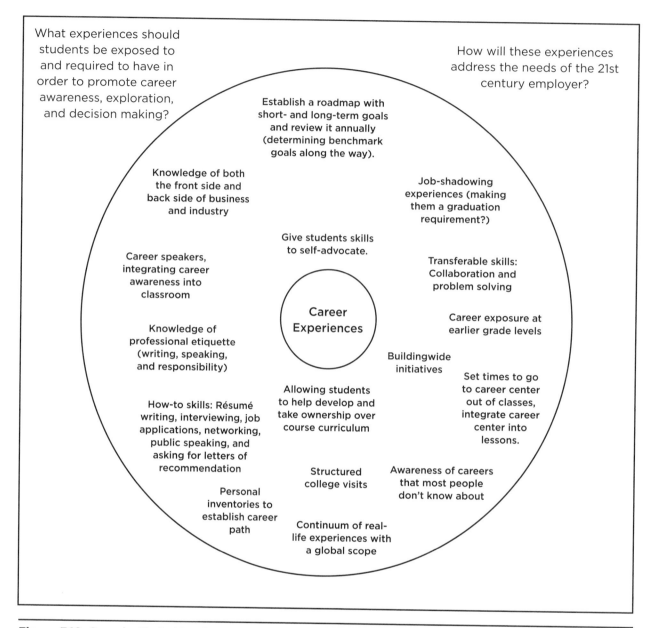

Figure 7.10: Sample Circle Map for student career experiences.

as a middle school educator, the principal invited parents to develop Circle Maps with information about their child while he did the same about his own five-year-old. In addition to allaying their concerns about him being a "middle school guy," the principal felt this activity had other benefits for him and the parents. "[This activity] allows me to teach the maps to parents," he said, "and explain that the Thinking Maps are a big part of how their children will be learning in our school. . . . They will be learning very quickly. . . . It really helped." Introducing the maps to the parents in this way immediately drew them into the culture of the school and connected them to their child's impending educational experience. Languages are a unifying feature in any culture. For parents to feel truly welcome in the school and empowered to become partners with the school in the education of their child, the principal understood that they, too, would have to learn to use this language.

Opportunities for professional development in the use of Thinking Maps in East Syracuse Minoa had extended to the school board level. Quite simply, members of the school board wanted to know what others knew. It was imperative that the use of Thinking Maps became part of their interactions and decision-making processes if they were truly to make a sustained, systemic transformation within the district. Introduced to the theory and practice of the maps, they learned the purpose of each map and the Frame of Reference and were shown examples of their use from all aspects of the system. Additionally, the board members received the opportunity to explore the application of the maps to school board–related topics as well as to topics meaningful in their personal lives. No entity of the system would remain on the sidelines. The use of the maps reached into all aspects of the school system's operations.

Perhaps the most affirming and powerful expression of Thinking Maps' impact on leading and learning at East Syracuse Minoa was students' proposal to implement a green campus. Using multiple Thinking Maps, a group of high school students developed a proposal for the school board to transform their campus into an environmentally responsible facility. At a school board meeting, the students made a public presentation of the plan, from inception to implementation. The plan impressed the board, and the school approved the proposal and supported the implementation of the project. Although occurring in the context of the educational system, this was indeed a real-world application. The students used the maps to generate their ideas, formulate their plan, and communicate their proposal to the school board. While they may have used Thinking Maps to develop an understanding of the content prior to the development of the proposal, students used them to skillfully and effectively communicate their ideas in a manner that could both educate and persuade a group of people in support of their project. Students clearly took Thinking Maps beyond the classroom in this example and used them in a manner that could easily be projected onto situations they will encounter beyond their formal schooling.

Achieving Clarity and Empowerment

In previous case studies, we included descriptions of interactions between teachers and administrators in which they used Thinking Maps to effectively facilitate high-quality supervisory and coaching interactions and sometimes salvage ones that appeared to have deteriorated beyond repair. The same experience repeated itself in East Syracuse Minoa as individuals used the maps in supervisory processes, resulting in both improvement and ending employment. In every instance, regardless of the outcome, the use of Thinking Maps enabled the participants to interact in a dignified and mutually respectful manner. Importantly, the maps helped the participants achieve a level of clarity that kept the focus on the salient questions around pedagogy and student learning.

In one instance that an administrator described, the performance-review process had become mired in generalities and was highly emotional for all involved. Although the system had defined the eight skill areas of a tenured teacher (figure 7.11), this particular teacher had not demonstrated evidence of improvement in these areas.

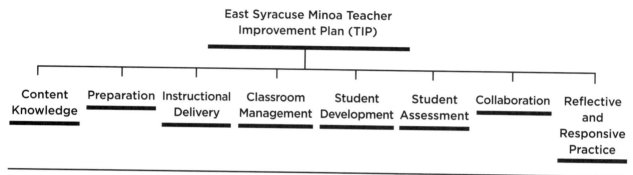

Figure 7.11: Sample Tree Map of the eight areas of a tenured teacher.

Attempts to communicate this to the teacher had been unsuccessful, and the lack of clarity compounded the frustration and anxiety that everyone involved in the process was experiencing. Power and authority now dominated the interaction where it needed mutuality and genuine dialogue. One of the senior administrators involved sat down with the principal and the teacher and created a Tree Map with the eight skill areas and the evidence from observations for each area. (See figure 7.12.)

The information was presented in a systematic way with all parties focusing their attention on the Tree Map. This simple act of shifting attention from the person to the practice, as displayed in the Tree Map, had a tangible influence on the interaction of those involved. As the senior administrator noted, "The meeting was much less emotional because it took the focus off the person and the personal and onto the issues and the evidence." Consequently, the reduction in tension at the meeting created space for dialogue to occur and ideas to be heard and understood in ways not previously possible. With the Tree Map as an external landscape to look at information more objectively, the teacher and administrators developed a constructive dialogue about the teacher's practice and designed steps to possibly improve the teacher's performance. They co-created another Tree Map (figure 7.13, page 136) as a roadmap to guide the teacher and the administrator in working together to improve the teacher's performance and consequently the learning experience of the students.

In this instance, the teacher worked hard to improve her performance, focusing on the areas identified through this process, and ultimately she received tenure. More importantly, the learning experience of the students in her class was elevated to the level the district valued. Had the maps not been used, this process would likely have continued to escalate in a negative direction and become contentious; and whether it resulted in tenure or dismissal, the damage to the culture of the system and the experience of the students would have been significant. Commenting on a similar process and the impact of using the maps on the

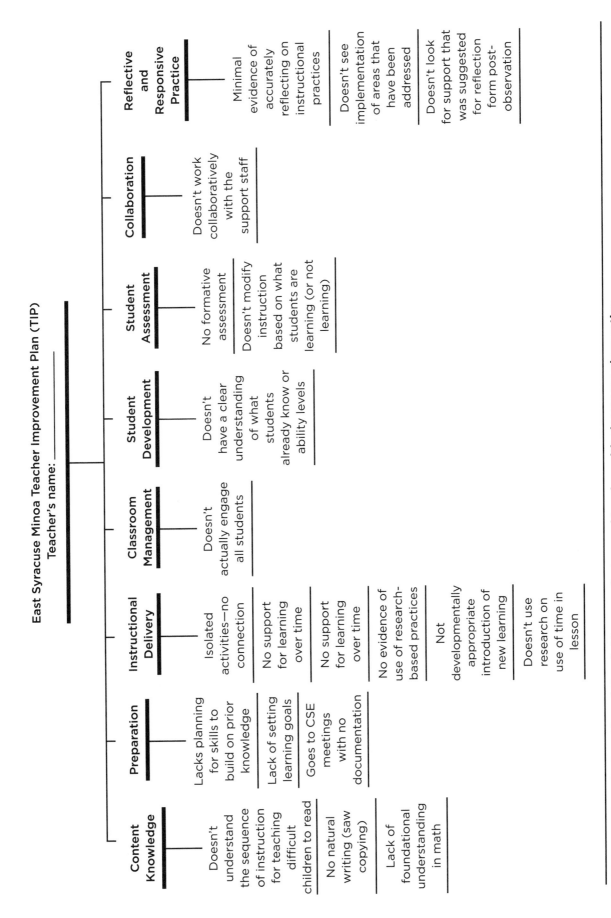

East Syracuse Minoa Teacher Improvement Plan (TIP)

Teacher's name: _____

Content Knowledge
- Doesn't understand the sequence of instruction for teaching difficult children to read
- No natural writing (saw copying)
- Lack of foundational understanding in math

Preparation
- Lacks planning for skills to build on prior knowledge
- Lack of setting learning goals
- Goes to CSE meetings with no documentation

Instructional Delivery
- Isolated activities—no connection
- No support for learning over time
- No support for learning over time
- No evidence of use of research-based practices
- Not developmentally appropriate introduction of new learning
- Doesn't use research on use of time in lesson

Classroom Management
- Doesn't actually engage all students

Student Development
- Doesn't have a clear understanding of what students already know or ability levels

Student Assessment
- No formative assessment
- Doesn't modify instruction based on what students are learning (or not learning)

Collaboration
- Doesn't work collaboratively with the support staff

Reflective and Responsive Practice
- Minimal evidence of accurately reflecting on instructional practices
- Doesn't see implementation of areas that have been addressed
- Doesn't look for support that was suggested for reflection form post-observation

Figure 7.12: Sample Tree Map of the eight areas of a tenured teacher with classroom observation.

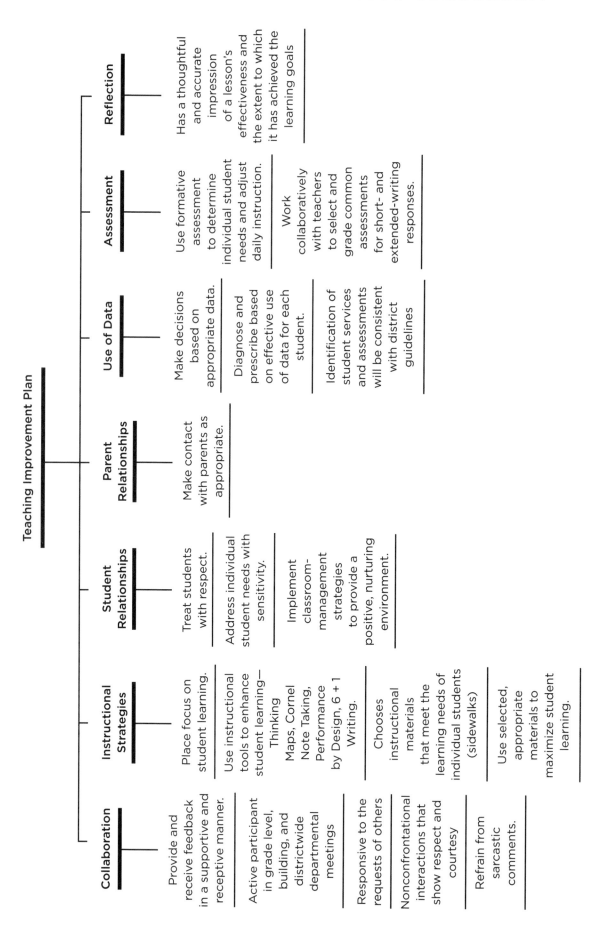

Figure 7.13: Sample Tree Map to improve teacher performance.

interaction between herself and a teacher, the middle school principal observed, "Putting the expectations into a Tree Map reduced the tension of the parties at the table because now the focus was on what needs to be done to achieve improvement. . . . What needs to be improved becomes more neutral." Reflecting further about the impact of the maps on this process as the third point in which the teacher and administrator literally join together in pursuit of mutual understanding, she continued, "[The Tree Map] gets the focus and takes away some of the personalization. . . . It doesn't feel like blame, shame, and intimidation. . . . It's much more objective and takes the emotionality out of it."

In response to threat and anxiety, the brain is often incapable of responding intelligently to information. Our emotions are powerful filters that can both inform and inhibit our ability to process information. Under perceived threat, the brain's primary responsibility is to protect us from danger—not ideal conditions for learning, but certainly necessary to secure our emotional and physical safety. Lack of clarity or threat of losing one's job can certainly produce anxiety. For the administrator involved as well as the teacher, this lack of clarity can influence how he or she approaches a sensitive interaction. One administrator commented, "The maps make it so you don't have to defend yourself; the maps make it so you don't have to go to that defensive place—it's so easy to escalate—there's no need to escalate." Another observed, "The maps provided clarity for me, and I was well prepared. . . . They helped me set the stage for the conversation; they helped me clarify." With the support of Thinking Maps, people are able to address complex issues and uncertain situations with the security of knowing that they have tools and strategies to help themselves and others achieve the clarity necessary to make informed, intelligent decisions.

Achieving Sustainability

At East Syracuse Minoa Central School District, the ethnographic data clearly show that the leaders, teachers, and students were committed to the successful use of Thinking Maps. Their use as a language for leading and learning was embedded in every facet of the system. As Donna DeSiato unequivocally stated, "Cultivating thinking is the focus of our work for learners at all levels."

One of the greatest threats to long-term sustainability at East Syracuse Minoa, like many schools, is the need for ongoing, high-quality faculty development and training. East Syracuse Minoa employed two very dedicated and well-trained Thinking Maps trainers to help those using the maps. However, those two trainers had many other obligations within the system. Recognizing the need for ongoing assistance to teachers and leaders, the district shifted one person's position to full-time responsibility for implementation of the maps.

At the end of our interview, one senior administrator was surprised to think that any aspect of East Syracuse Minoa's culture change was very special. She remarked, "You just kind of do it. . . . I definitely feel a shift and change for the better, but it takes time to see those dramatic differences—although everything is improving, our graduation rates, our test scores—although not quite as much as we'd like to see yet. . . . It takes time."

Additionally, as she pointed out, most teachers had, at the time of these interviews, only been using Thinking Maps for two years and the administrators a bit less. Nonetheless, she acknowledged that major shifts were already happening.

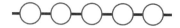

When you change the language of a place, you change the culture. When you change the culture to improve learning for adults and children, amazing things can happen. East Syracuse Minoa saw those changes. Test scores improved, as did high school graduation and college acceptance. All the schools observed for this ethnography had a feeling of individual and collective efficacy—that comes when all leaders understand each other, feel equipped to skillfully fulfill their responsibility to the system, and work collaboratively toward a common goal—improving learning for all students. As Superintendent Donna DeSiato stated:

> As we strengthen our learning organization, these tools enhance critical thinking, problem solving, collaborating, and communicating. Thinking Maps support our commitment to continuous improvement, striving for excellence in all areas of performance as we prepare our graduates for the 21st century.

EPILOGUE
Thinking by Design: The Act of Leading Thinkers

Despite David Brooks's (2008) contention that we are currently in the *cognitive age* (see page 112), perhaps we have always been there. Each generation affords itself the conceit of thinking we are at a place where others have never been before. Yet it's almost impossible to imagine a time in which thinking and the ability to do so skillfully and artfully were not necessary and important to our survival and fulfillment. What has changed, however, is the hyperconnectivity of the world in which we live, making agile and effective thinking a more urgently needed skill. Information abounds, not only in places like the Internet, but in the minds of people. Very few of us enter a meeting uninformed.

Doctors have become accustomed to their patients knowing as much about their condition as the doctor, or at least having an abundant amount of information about it at their disposal. Knowledge is power, presumably, but as Paulo Freire (2000) contends, "Liberating education consists of *acts of cognition*, not transferals of information" (p. 79). Such acts of cognition or meaning making are what ultimately transform information into actionable knowledge and give agency to the individual. So maybe Brooks was correct, stating that the most important part of information's journey was "the last few inches," the time and space it travels to and through the brain, where we have the opportunity to transform that information into knowledge (Brooks, 2008). Ultimately, an act of cognition will determine how useful that information will become in helping us address the complex challenges in today's rapidly and constantly changing world.

Leading thinkers, then, is an act of affirmation and belief in the potential that exists within all people to contribute to and lead the decision-making processes so critical to the success of schools. The school itself exists as a physical structure. The work of the school occurs through the people within it. Embracing this and acting in ways to enhance and optimize the ability of people to think and perform at highly effective levels must be the greatest priority of leadership.

The leaders we met in the course of this study all recognized that they could not achieve such clarity in their thinking or develop such efficacy in dealing with complex situations alone. The ability of their schools to adapt to new circumstances, to thrive in their ability to meet the needs of their students, and to fulfill their missions required collaboration and a commitment to nurturing each other's potential to think and act skillfully. In Thinking Maps, they found a common and universal language for thinking connectively, displaying the richness of these thought patterns, and uniting people in the pursuit of shared purpose and coordinated action. The use of the maps networked people and ideas and created a dynamic interconnectedness rich in possibilities.

In each setting we studied, we observed what organizational theorist Etienne Wenger (1998) describes as a *community of practice* being built. Involving mutual engagement, joint enterprise, and a shared repertoire of routines, tacit rules of conduct, and knowledge, communities of practice, as such, are self-generating and sustainable. Thinking Maps evidently contributed to the development of these communities of practice at each of the three levels. Their use empowered individuals and was an agent for collaborative work. The clarity and efficiency they afforded members of the school community in their interactions with each other and in their own reflective processes facilitated the development of shared purpose and focused action. Additionally, as a common visual language for thinking, the maps reflected a core value of the school community and continued to shape it in that way as well. As Fritjof Capra (2002) observes, "Ideally, the formal organization recognizes and supports its informal networks of relationships and incorporates their innovations into its structures" (pp. 110–111). Used in both formal and informal contexts, in meetings, and by individuals for their own reflective processes, Thinking Maps permeated the school environment. Their use became a *cognitive bridge*, stimulating and enhancing what Capra (2002) describes as the "continuous interplay between its informal networks and its formal structures" (p. 110).

Taking the lead at this time in our educational history means leading thinkers within the adult educational community as well as our students. The new globalized technological world of communication networks requires us to learn about, practice, reflect on, and explicitly stretch our own range of thinking processes as patterns. We must set this expectation for ourselves as we have now pronounced loud and clear the need to focus on high-order thinking, questioning, and products of thinking *for our students*.

A common refrain from adults about this generation is that its members' multitasking minds scatter ideas in the Ethernet blizzard and remain snowblinded by the incapacity to focus. This generation, they fear, is disabled by inattention, hooked up to so many technologies, and overwhelmed by huge amounts of tangled information. For students who now have access to so much information (that we can't control) as they download full texts, movies, and music to their handheld computers in the back of the classroom, we as educators have become *just one of the models* for our students as they moment-to-moment multitask via the web. Just a generation ago, we could distribute textbooks to students at the beginning of the year and know that they had few other avenues for accessing information and distributing their attention. They would focus on the text. Now they *create* hundreds of texts per day via a system of dynamic social-networking sites.

We may need to reframe our challenge then: can we be adaptive to the immediate needs of students who are challenged not in their ability to access and download whole textbooks in a matter of moments but in their ability to think through this information and make sense of this new networked world?

The themes of this book may apply to how we think about students and what we focus on in schools: can our students think with *clarity, efficiency,* and fluidity in *collaborative* teams so they are *empowered* rather than overwhelmed by streams of information and data, providing a new foundation for decisions that sustain them as individuals and support them in leading *sustainable* schools and communities for their children of the next generation? Let's listen to ourselves as we make the direct link between leading and learning. In the 21st century, we state that highly innovative, high-order thinkers who can problem solve and make thoughtful decisions must be the outcome of the educational process, and that leaders must also develop and model these same qualities. In the school communities we studied in which individuals used Thinking Maps at all levels, the common use of this visual language for thinking made an explicit and inherent connection between the informal and formal structures that guided and determined their actions. Leaders in each of these settings—superintendents, principals, teacher leaders, coaches, and so on—valued the individual and collective intelligence of those with whom they worked. In choosing to use Thinking Maps as the organizational language for their schools, these leaders aligned their practice with their belief that thinking *is* the foundation for leading and learning. In doing so, they led thinkers to create thinking schools for the purpose of explicitly engaging and developing *thinking students*.

REFERENCES AND RESOURCES

Alper, L., & Hyerle, D. (2007). *Thinking Maps: A language for leadership.* Cary, NC: Thinking Maps.

Anderson, L. W., Krathwohl, D. R., Airasian, P. W., Cruishank, K. A., Mayer, R. M., et al. (Eds.). (2001). *A taxonomy for learning, teaching, and assessing: A revision of Bloom's taxonomy of educational objectives.* New York: Longman.

Bloom, B. S. (1986). The hands and feet of genius: Automaticity. *Educational Leadership, 43*(5), 70–77.

Bolman, L. G., & Deal, T. E. (1997). *Reframing organizations: Artistry, choice, and leadership* (2nd ed.). San Francisco: Jossey-Bass.

Brooks, D. (2008, May 2). The cognitive age. *New York Times.* Accessed at www.nytimes.com/2008/05/02/opinion/02brooks.html on March 31, 2011.

Bryant, A. (2010, February 21). Xerox's new chief tries to redefine its culture. *The New York Times*, p. BU1.

Capra, F. (1996). The web of life: A new scientific understanding of living systems. New York: Random House.

Capra, F. (2002). *The hidden connection: Integrating the biological, cognitive, and social dimensions of life into a science of sustainability.* New York: Random House.

Cohen, D. H. (1973). *The learning child: Guidelines for parents and teachers.* New York: Vintage Books.

Costa, A. L. (Ed.). (2001). *Developing minds: A resource book for teaching thinking* (3rd ed.). Alexandria, VA: Association for Supervision and Curriculum Development.

Costa, A. L. (2008a). *The school as a home for the mind: Creating mindful curriculum, instruction, and dialogue.* Thousand Oaks, CA: Corwin Press.

Costa, A. L. (2008b). The thought-filled curriculum. *Educational Leadership, 65*(5), 20–24.

Costa, A. L., & Kallick, B. (2000). *Discovering and exploring habits of mind.* Alexandria, VA: Association for Supervision and Curriculum Development.

Danielson, C. (1996). *Enhancing professional practice: A framework for teaching.* Alexandria, VA: Association for Supervision and Curriculum Development.

Darling-Hammond, L. (2010). *The flat world and education: How America's commitment to equity will determine our future.* New York: Teachers College Press.

Davis, S., Darling-Hammond, L., LaPoint, M., & Meyerson, D. (2005). *School leadership study: Developing successful principals* [Research Report]. Stanford, CA: Stanford Educational Leadership Institute. Accessed at http://seli.stanford.edu/research/sls.htm on December 15, 2010.

DeSiato, D., & Morgan, J. (in press). *Thinking: The essential ingredient for success in the 21st century.* Thousand Oaks, CA: Corwin Press.

Dewey, J. (1998). *Experience and education* (60th anniversary ed.). West Lafayette, IN: Kappa Delta Pi.

Dickmann, M. H., & Stanford-Blair, N. (2002). *Connecting leadership to the brain.* Thousand Oaks, CA: Corwin Press.

Dickmann, M. H., & Stanford-Blair, N. (2009). *Mindful leadership: A brain-based framework* (2nd ed.). Thousand Oaks, CA: Corwin Press.

Duckworth, E. (2006). *The having of wonderful ideas and other essays on teaching and learning* (3rd ed.). New York: Teachers College Press.

DuFour, R. (2004). What is a professional learning community? *Educational Leadership, 61*(8), 6–11.

DuFour, R., DuFour, R., Eaker, R., & Many, T. (2006). *Learning by doing: A handbook for professional learning communities at work.* Bloomington, IN: Solution Tree Press.

East Syracuse Minoa Central School District. (n.d.). Vision, mission, & beliefs. Accessed at www.esmschools.org/district.cfm?subpage=24329 on July 8, 2011.

East Syracuse Minoa Central School District. (2009, October). *Community engagement: A model for 21st century learning.* Paper presented at the 90th Annual Convention and Trade Show of the New York State School Boards Association, New York. Accessed at www.nyssba.org/clientuploads/nyssba_pdf/PrintOnDemand/Saturday/Community%20 Engagement%20A%20Model%20for%2021st%20Century%20Learning.pdf on July 8, 2011.

Ernst, K. (2011). Coaching and supervising reflective practice. In D. N. Hyerle & L. Alper (Eds.), *Student successes with Thinking Maps* (2nd ed., pp. 178–191). Thousand Oaks, CA: Corwin Press.

Ernst, K. (in press). *Visible coaching and supervision.* Thousand Oaks, CA: Corwin Press.

Eskew, M. (2005, December). *Education in an age of globalization.* Speech presented at the States Institute on International Education in the Schools, Washington, DC. Accessed at www.ncssfl.org/Eskew-Speech.doc on July 12, 2011.

Freire, P. (2000). *Pedagogy of the oppressed* (30th anniversary ed.). New York: Continuum International.

Friedman, T. L. (2005). *The world is flat: A brief history of the twenty-first century.* New York: Farrar, Straus and Giroux.

Fullan, M. (1993). *Change forces: Probing the depths of educational reform.* London: Falmer Press.

Fullan, M. (1999). *Change forces: The sequel.* Philadelphia: Falmer Press.

Fullan, M. (2001a). *Leading in a culture of change.* San Francisco: Jossey-Bass.

Fullan, M. (2001b). *The new meaning of educational change* (3rd ed.). New York: Teachers College Press

Fullan, M. (2003). *Change forces with a vengeance.* London: RoutledgeFalmer.

Fullan, M. (2010). *Motion leadership: The skinny on becoming change savvy.* Thousand Oaks, CA: Corwin Press.

Galagan, P. A. (1991). The learning organization made plain: An interview with Peter Senge. *American Society Training & Development, 45*(10), 37–44.

Gardner, H. (1995). *Leading minds.* New York: Basic Books.

Gardner, H. (2006). *Five minds for the future.* Boston: Harvard Business School.

Glaser, M. (2008). *Drawing is thinking.* New York: Overlook Duckworth, Mayer.

Glickman, C. D. (1993). *Renewing America's schools: Guide for school-based action.* San Francisco: Jossey-Bass.

Goleman, D. (1985). *Vital lies, simple truths: The psychology of self-deception.* New York: Simon & Schuster.

Goleman, D., Boyatzis, R., & McKee, A. (2002). *Primal leadership: Realizing the power of emotional intelligence.* Boston: Harvard Business School Press.

Greene, M. (1995). *Releasing the imagination: Essays on education, the arts, and social change.* San Francisco: Jossey-Bass.

Hall, G. (2005). Interview with Peter M. Senge and Otto Scharmer. *ASTD Links.* Accessed at www.presence.net/pdf/ASTD_InPerson_Senge_Scharmer.pdf on December 20, 2009.

Hargreaves, A., & Fink, D. (2003). Sustaining leadership. In B. Davies & J. West-Burnham (Eds.), *Handbook of educational leadership and management* (pp. 435–450). London: Pearson Education.

Holzman, S. (2011). A first language for thinking in a multi-lingual school. In D. N. Hyerle & L. Alper (Eds.), *Student successes with Thinking Maps* (2nd ed., pp. 118–125). Thousand Oaks, CA: Corwin Press.

Hord, S. M. (1997). *Professional learning communities: Communities of continuous inquiry and improvement.* Austin, TX: Southwest Educational Development Laboratory.

Hyerle, D. (2009). *Visual tools for transforming information into knowledge.* Thousand Oaks, CA: Corwin Press.

Hyerle, D., & Alper, L. (2006). *Thinking Maps: A language for leadership.* Cary, NC: Thinking Maps.

Hyerle, D., & Alper, L. (Eds.). (2011). *Student successes with Thinking Maps* (2nd ed.). Thousand Oaks, CA: Corwin Press.

Hyerle, D., & Yeager, C. (2007). *Thinking Maps: A language for learning.* Cary, NC: Thinking Maps.

Jaworski, J., & Flowers, B. (1998). *Synchronicity: The inner path of leadership.* San Francisco: Berrett-Koehler.

Kotter, J. (1996). *Leading change.* Boston: Harvard Business School Press.

Lakoff, G. (1980). *Metaphors we live by.* Chicago: University of Chicago Press.

Lambert, L. (1998). *Building leadership capacity in schools.* Alexandria, VA: Association for Supervision and Curriculum Development.

Lambert, L. G. (2007). Lasting leadership: Toward sustainable school improvement. *Journal of Educational Change, 8,* 311–322.

Lambert, L. (2009). Reconceptualizing the road toward leadership capacity. In A. Blankenship, P. D. Houston, & R. W. Cole (Eds.), *Building sustainable leadership capacity* (pp. 7–28). Thousand Oaks, CA: Corwin Press.

Lambert, L., Walker, D., Zimmerman, D. P., Cooper, J. E., Lambert, M. D., et al. (Eds.). (1995). *The constructivist leader.* New York: Teachers College Press.

Leithwood, K., Seashore Louis, K., Anderson, S., & Wahlstrom, K. (2004). *How leadership influences student learning* [Research Report]. St. Paul, MN: Center for Applied Research and Educational Improvement.

Martin-Kniep, G. O. (2008). *Communities that learn, lead, and last: Building and sustaining educational expertise.* San Francisco: Jossey-Bass.

Marzano, R. J., Pickering, D. J., & Pollock, J. E. (2001). *Classroom instruction that works: Research-based strategies for increasing student achievement.* Alexandria, VA: Association for Supervision and Curriculum Development.

Marzano, R. J., Waters, T., & McNulty, B. A. (2005). *School leadership that works: From research to results.* Alexandria, VA: Association for Supervision and Curriculum Development.

Piaget, J., & Inhelder, B. (1969). *The psychology of the child.* New York: Basic Books.

Pink, D. (2006). *A whole new mind: Moving from the information age to the conceptual age.* New York: Berkley.

Saposnick, K. (2000). Collaboration is key to organizational change: An interview with Peter Senge. *Leverage Points, 34.* Accessed at www.pegasuscom.com/levpoints/sengeint .html on June 26, 2011.

Schön, D. (1987). *Educating the reflective practitioner.* San Francisco: Jossey-Bass.

Senge, P. M. (1990a). *The fifth discipline: The art and practice of the learning organization.* New York: Doubleday.

Senge, P. M. (1990b). The leader's new work: Building learning organizations. *Sloan Management Review, 32*(1), 7–22

Senge, P., Scharmer, O. C., Jaworski, J., & Flowers, B. S. (2004). *Presence: Human purpose and the field of the future.* Cambridge, MA: The Society for Organizational Learning.

Senge, P., Smith, B., Kruschwitz, N., Laur, J., & Schley, S. (2010). *The necessary revolution: Working together to create a sustainable world.* New York: Broadway Books.

Thinking Foundation. (n.d.a). *Mr. K shares how Thinking Maps open up interactive student driven discussions* [Video]. Lyme, NH: Author. Accessed at www.thinkingfoundation.org /video/clips/norman-howard-mr-k.html on July 6, 2011.

Thinking Foundation. (n.d.b). *Norman Howard School: From students to leadership to school board* [Video]. Lyme, NH: Author. Accessed at www.thinkingfoundation.org/video/clips /norman-howard-leadership.html on July 6, 2011.

Thinking Foundation. (n.d.c). *Thinking Maps and school effectiveness: A study of a UK comprehensive school report.* Lyme, NH: Author. Accessed at www.thinkingfoundation.org /research/case_studies/st-roberts/pdf/st_robert_case_study.pdf on July 6, 2011.

Thinking Foundation. (n.d.d). *Thinking Maps, thinking teams, thinking schools: Using Thinking Maps as a catalyst for strengthening school-wide leadership and increasing communication that will lead to improved student learning outcomes.* Lyme, NH: Author. Accessed at www .thinkingfoundation.org/research/case_studies/blackham/blackham_bridgeport.html on July 6, 2011.

Wagner, T. (2008). *The global achievement gap: Why even our best schools don't teach the new survival skills our children need—and what we can do about it.* New York: Basic Books.

Wagner, T., Kegan, R., Lahey, L., Lemons, R. W., Garnier, J., et al. (2006). *Change leadership: A practical guide to transforming our schools.* San Francisco: Jossey-Bass.

Wasserman, G., & Gallegos, P. V. (2007). *Engaging diversity: Disorienting dilemmas that transform relationships.* Accessed at www.icwconsulting.com/pdf/ICW-Article -WassermanGallegos-2007.pdf on March 2, 2009.

Wasserman, G., Gallegos, P. V., & Ferdman, B. M. (2006). Dancing with resistance: Leadership challenges in fostering a culture of inclusion. In K. Thomas (Ed.), *Diversity resistance in organizations: Manifestations and solutions* (pp. 175–200). Mahwah, NJ: Erlbaum.

Wenger, E. (1998). Communities of practice: Learning as a social system. *Systems Thinker, 9*(5). Accessed at www.co-i-l.com/coil/knowledge-garden/cop/lss.shtml on July 8, 2011.

Wheatley, M. (1999). *Leadership and the new sciences: Discovering order in a chaotic world.* San Francisco: Berrett-Koehler.

Wheatley, M. (2005*). Finding our way: Leadership for an uncertain time.* San Francisco: Berrett-Koehler.

Zimmerman, D. (1995). The linguistics of leadership. In L. Lambert, D. Walker, D. P. Zimmerman, J. E. Cooper, M. D. Lambert, et al. (Eds.), *The constructivist leader* (pp. 104–120). New York: Teachers College Press.

INDEX

An f represents a figure, and a t represents a table.

A

Academic Excellence and Rigor Action Team, 125, 128t, 130
accountability, 120
acts of cognition, 139
administration, and Thinking Maps, 6, 18, 30, 46, 50–51, 54. *See also* collaborative thinking case study
    on effect on teacher development, 96–97
    in systems thinking case study, 115, 125–126, 134, 137–138
advanced cues, 115
Anderson, S., 28
anxiety, 40, 52, 102, 134, 137. *See also* emotions
Aristotle, 25
Arthur, B., 36
automaticity, 6

B

balanced leadership framework, 29–30
beliefs, x, 15
    alignment with actions, 27, 40, 45, 119
    shared, 29, 39, 72
best practices, nine (Marzano), 16
Bloom, B. S., 5, 6, 16
Bloom's revised taxonomy, 5, 16
Bluebonnet Elementary School, x–xi, 86–88
Bolman, L. G., 31–32, 39, 74
Bond, N., 78–80
book study Tree Map, 89f
Boyatzis, R., 39
Brace Map
    defining, 7f
    to describe school and influence on student performance, 14f

Bridge Map
    defining, 7f
    to describe learning in 21st century, 15f
Bridgeport Public Schools, 91
Brooks, D., 112, 139
Bubble Map
    defining, 7f
    of high student performance, 13f
    of NQT's experience using Thinking Maps, 61f
    of qualities of Thinking Maps, 17f
    of traditional feedback method, 56f
Burns, U., 107

C

Campbell, J., 85
Canisteo-Greenwood Central School District, x, 69–83
Capra, F., 75, 140
career expectations, student, 132f
change, eight forces of (Fullan), 109–110
Change Leadership Group at the Harvard Graduate School of Education, 111
Circle Map
    to define mission of school, 92f
    defining, 7f
    to establish team norms, 71f
    to identify needs in RTI process, 79f
    to improve school and community communication, 129f
    of low student performance, 12f
    to record meeting expectations, 100f
    of student career expectations, 132f
clarity dimension of leadership, 9, 26f–27, 48–52, 85–86, 104, 105, 107–108, 140
coaching case study. *See* Newly Qualified Teachers (NQTs) case study;

professional artistry case study

cognitive age, 15f, 112, 139

cognitive bridge, 140

cognitive connections, 3

cognitive development, 55, 62, 110–111, 112

cognitive neuroscience, 3

cognitive overload, 3

cognitive universality, 36

Cohen, D., 87

collaboration dimension of leadership, 9, 26f, 27, 47, 86, 104, 105, 107–108. *See also* collaborative thinking case study

collaborative culture, 27, 62, 118

collaborative environment, 45–46

collaborative problem solving, 118–119. *See also* collaborative thinking case study and districtwide learning community case study

collaborative thinking case study, 69–83

  fostering collaborative thinking, 118–119

  leadership training for, 72–75

  professional learning communities (PLCs), 75–78

  sustainable plan, 78–81

  Thinking Maps as glue, 81–83

  vision sharing, 70–72

common formative assessment (CFA), 96

communication, school and community, 129f

communication issues, in schoolwide thinking case study, 94, 96, 98–105

Communications, Systems, and Structures Action Team, 129, 130

community of practice, 140

Connecticut Accountability for Learning Initiative (CALI), 90–91

Connecticut Mastery Test (CMT), 96

connective leadership, common themes in, 9–10f, 107–108, 203

consciousness, capacity for, 86

contextual knowledge, 30f

Costa, A., 16, 53, 106

cues, advanced, 115

culture

  collaborative, 27, 62, 118

  hierarchical, 45, 87

  inclusive, 33

  of inquiry, 33, 117

  school, 10, 39

D

Daily 5 (literacy strategy), 87

Danielson, C., 53

Darling-Hammond, L., 28–29, 111

Davis, S., 28–29, 31

Deal, T. E., 31–32, 39, 74

declarative knowledge, 30f

DeSiato, D., x, 109, 113–116, 118, 119, 127, 137, 138

Dewey, J., 53

Dickmann, M., 36, 86, 107, 108

disconnection, sense of, 1, 3

distributive leadership, 91–94

districtwide learning community case study, 113–138

  clarity issues, 133–134, 137

  community formation, 127, 129–133

  empowerment issues, 134

  leadership challenges, 117–118

  meeting productivity, 119–123

  research-informed decision making, 115–116

  shift in discourse, 118–119

  strategic plan for, 123–127, 125f, 126f

  sustainability issues, 137–138

diversity, engaging in, 33–34f

Double Bubble Map

  to analyze guided-reading program per grade level, 103f

  to compare student performance, 14f

  comparing PLCs and strategic school plan, 76f

  defining, 7f

  for NQT training, 58f

  for parent engagement, 131f

Duckworth, E., 28

E

East Syracuse Minoa Central School District, x, 109, 113–138

ecological communities, 75

efficacy, 17, 72, 74, 118, 138, 139

efficiency, 32, 91

efficiency dimension of leadership, 9, 26f, 27, 86, 105, 107–108, 120, 140

eight leadership practices (Fullan), 16

eight levels of change (Kotter), 16

emotional hijack, 106

emotions, 50, 51–52, 105–107

    anxiety, 40, 52, 102, 134, 137

empathy, 2, 15, 23, 110, 112

empowerment

    in relationships, 47, 67, 68

    of students, 29

empowerment dimension of leadership, 9, 26f, 27–28, 105, 107–108, 140

empowerment issues

    in collaborative thinking case study, 83

    in districtwide learning community case study, 122, 133, 134

    in schoolwide thinking case study, 87, 98, 102–105, 106

end-of-the-year orientation, 82–83

equity, 63

Ernst, K., 62–67

Eskew, M., 107–108

evaluation and benchmarking Tree Map, 20f

experiential knowledge, 30f

externalization, 45, 56, 104

F

feedback, 50, 54–55

    high quality, 115

    sustainable, 87

    traditional, 55, 56f

    using Thinking Maps, 61f

fight-or-flight, 106

Fink, D., 35

five disciplines of systems thinking (Senge), 16, 110

fixity, illusion of, 107–108

Florence E. Blackham School, xi, 88–96, 97–98

Flowers, B., 35

Flow Map

    defining, 7f

    of description of day of low-performing student, 15f

    of grievance, 48f

    of intervention meeting process, 81f

    of math-lesson observation, 64f

    of REAL model, 34f

    of task force responsibilities and procedures, 21f

    of team agenda, 94f

    of Thinking Maps training, 42f

four Cs, 127

Frame of Reference, 6

    for collaborative thinking, 69

    defining, 7f, 40

    for defining guidance counselor roles, 121f

    for leadership themes, 26f

    for learning relationships, 87

    for school mission, 92f

    for student performance, 15

Franklin Elementary School in New York, xi

Freire, P., 139

Fullan, M., 6, 16, 69, 87, 109–110

G

Gardner, H., 40, 110, 111, 112

generative listening, 106

Glaser, M., 1, 3, 49, 51, 106–107

Glickman, C., 127

Goleman, D., 2, 39, 52, 68, 106

graphic organizers, 17, 106

green campus, 133

Greene, M., 48

grievance situation case study, 41, 43–47, 48f

guidance counselors, 120–122f, 121f

guided-reading program, 101–102, 103f

guiding questions, 81–82, 87

H

habits of mind, sixteen (Costa), 16

Hall, G., 35–36
Hargreaves, A., 35
Henderson, S., 43, 45, 46, 47
hierarchical culture, 45, 87
hierarchy of needs, 32
higher-order questions, 115, 140
Holzman, S., 96–97, 98
Hord, S., 118
Horizontal Data Teams, 90, 91, 93, 94, 96, 97
"how" question, 8–9
human capacity, of leaders, 36

I

illusion of fixity, 107–108
inclusive culture, 33
information age, 15f
inquiry, culture of, 33, 117
intermediate zones of practice, 53
intervention meeting process, 81f

J

Jaworski, J., 35, 107

K

Kantor, J., xi, 49–51, 86
Kay, K., 127
King, M., 25
knowledge, for school leaders, 30
Kotter, J., 16

L

Lambert, L., x, 32–33, 75, 87, 88, 107, 117
LaPoint, M., 28–29
leaders. See also leadership; leadership themes
    and human capacity, 36
    qualities of effective, 28–29
leadership
    balanced leadership framework, 29–30
    broadening scope of, 35–36
    building leadership capacity, 32–33
    connective, common themes in, 9–10f, 107–108, 203
    defining and understanding leadership role, 31

distributive, 91–94
and diversity, 33–34
key leadership frames, 31–32t
meeting outcomes, 100–102
and organizational change, 34–35
resonant, 106
service, 91–94
sustaining successful, 35
Thinking Maps as language for, 16–22
leadership practices, eight (Fullan), 16
leadership team meeting Thinking Map, 41, 43f–44
leadership themes. See also Frame of Reference
    clarity, 9, 26f–27, 48–52, 85–86, 104, 105, 107–108, 140, 285–286
    collaboration, 9, 26f, 27, 47, 86, 104, 105, 107–108
    efficiency, 9, 26f, 27, 86, 105, 107–108, 120, 140
    empowerment, 9, 26f, 27–28, 105, 107–108, 140
    sustainability, 9, 26f, 28, 105, 107–108
leading as learning, 110–111
learning organizations, 10, 33, 34, 71, 110, 118
Leithwood, K., 28
LeVita, C., 31
listening, generative, 106

M

Martin-Kniep, G. O., 39
Marzano, R. J., 16, 29–30, 115, 116
math-lesson observation, 64f, 65f, 66f
Matteson, J., x, 69–83
McDermott, V., 9–10, 106
McGuire, K., x–xi, 86–88
McKee, A., 39
McNulty, B. A., 29–30
metamap, 15
Meyerson, D., 28–29
Mills, R., 116
mission statement, 92f, 113–114f, 115
Morgan, J., x, 9, 109, 116, 118, 119, 124–125, 127

Mr. K, 21–22, 110
Multi-Flow Map
   defining, 7f
   of leadership team meeting, 43f
   of leadership themes, 26f
   of low student performance, 11f
   of math-lesson observation, 65f
   partial map for NQT training, 57f
   of team mission, 95f
multitasking, 140

N

Neveldine, T., 118
Newly Qualified Teachers (NQTs) case study,
      54–62
   Double Bubble Map for training, 58f
   feedback using Thinking Maps, 61f
   partial map for training, 57f
   traditional feedback, 55, 56f
   Tree Maps for teacher performance, 59f, 60f
New York State Regents Exam, 21
nine best practices (Marzano), 16
Norman Howard School, 18–22, 23, 110

O

organizational change, disciplines of, 34–35
organizers, 17, 106, 115

P

parent engagement, 130–133, 131f
Piaget, J., 5
Pink, D., 110–111, 112
PowerPoint, 19
procedural knowledge, 30f
process benefit of Thinking Maps, 86–87
professional artistry case study, 53–54, 62–67
   math-lesson observation, 64f, 65f, 66f
professional development. *See also* Newly
         Qualified Teachers (NQTs) case
         study; professional artistry case study;
         schoolwide thinking case study
   Thinking Maps training, ix, 6, 42f, 54, 115–
         116, 137

professional learning communities (PLCs),
      75–78
purpose and benefit of Thinking Maps, 86–87

Q

questions
   guiding, 81–82, 87
   higher-order, 115, 140
   "how" question, 8–9
   reflective, 67
   shifting, to foster collaboration, 118–119

R

reading, guided, 101–102, 103f
REAL model, 33–34f
reciprocity, 45, 67, 68, 75, 87, 88, 107
reflective practice, 53–54, 62–63, 65–67
reflective questions, 67
resonant leadership, 106
response to intervention (RTI), 79f, 82
Roberts, M., 18–21, 22, 23, 110

S

Sampson, M., x, 41–43, 46–47
Scharmer, O., 35–36
schemas, 2, 4, 15
Schön, D., 53
school and community communication, 129f
school boards, use of Thinking Maps, 21, 22,
      72, 82, 133
school culture, 10, 39
School to College and Career Advisory Board,
      130
schoolwide thinking case study, 88–98
   analysis and reflection, 90–91
   communication issues, 94, 96, 98–105
   distributive leadership and, 91–94
   empowerment development, 102–105
   leadership meeting outcomes, 100–102
   learning outcomes and, 96–98
Seashore Louis, K., 28
Sedgwick Central School District, x, 41–45,
      46–47
self-assessment, student, 8

Senge, P., 16, 28, 34–35, 36, 40, 70, 71, 110, 111, 112
service leadership, 91–94
simplexity, 6
sixteen habits of mind (Costa), 16
skillful thinking, developing, 54–62
SMART goals, 96, 97
software, Thinking Maps, ix, 12, 82
Southwell, K., 125, 127
Standford-Blair, N., 36, 86, 107, 108
strategic plan
    comparing PLCs and, 75, 76f
    for improving student achievement, 72, 74f
    for 21st century learning community, 123–127, 125f, 126f
    using multiple Thinking Maps, 73f
St. Robert of Newminster Catholic School and Sixth Form College, 54–62
student performance, 10–16. *See also* districtwide learning community case study
    Frame of Reference for, 15
    Thinking Maps for, 10–15, 97–98
students
    empowerment of, 29
    identifying needs of, 80f
    self-assessment by, 8
    special needs, 18–22, 23, 110
sustainability dimension of leadership, 9, 26f, 28, 105, 107–108
systems thinking, five disciplines of (Senge), 16, 110
systems thinking, in 21st century. *See also* districtwide learning community case study
    context of, 109–112

T

task force responsibilities and procedures, 21f
teacher effectiveness, enhancing, 53–54
teacher performance
    Newly Qualified Teachers, 54–62
    tenured teacher, 134–137
team agenda, 94f

team mission, 95f
technology age, 15f
tenured teacher performance case study, 134–137
    skill areas, 134f
    skill areas, classroom observation, 135f
Theory of the U, 36
Thinking Foundation website, 54
Thinking Maps. *See also* individual maps
    as assessment tools, 22
    basic qualities of, 16–17f
    cognitive processes of, 4–8
    connection to and difference from leadership theory, 16–18
    definitions of, 7f
    as language, 4
    as language for connective knowing, 22–23
    as language for leadership, 16–22
    process benefit of, 86–87
    purpose benefit of, 86–87
    teaching students about, 6, 8
    training leaders and teachers about, ix, 6, 42f, 54, 115–116, 137
    transferability of, 22
    value of, 16, 18
    verbal-visual patterns in, 5
    visual representation in, 8–9
Thinking Maps: A Language for Leadership (Alper and Hyerle), ix, 8
Thinking Maps: A Language for Learning (Hyerle and Yeager), ix
time issues, 10–11, 27, 119–120
transformational stage of development, 8
transparency, x, 15, 16, 55, 63, 67, 85, 96
Tree Map
    Academic Excellence and Rigor Action Team, 128t
    to analyze grade-level challenges, 101f
    of book study, 89f
    of common themes in connective leadership, 10f
    defining, 7f
    for defining guidance counselor roles, 122f

to describe performance of different
students, 14f
to describe teacher performance, 59f, 60f
of evaluation and benchmarking, 20f
of goals of strategic plan, 126f
to identify student needs, 80f
to improve teacher performance, 136f
of main areas of strategic plan, 125f
of math-lesson observation, 66f
of school mission, 90f, 114f
of skill areas of tenured teacher, 134f
of skill areas of tenured teacher, classroom
observation, 135f
of Thinking Maps implementation, 44f
trust, 33, 40, 41, 62, 63, 67, 105

values, x, 15
alignment with actions, 27, 40
core, 27, 40, 72, 74f, 82
shared, 39
Vertical Data Teams, xi, 90–91, 93–94, 96,
97–98, 100, 105

Wagner, T., 16, 39, 111–112
Wahlstrom, K., 28
Waters, T., 29–30
well-being, emotional, 1
Wenger, E., 140
Wheatley, M., 1, 67
Williams, L., x–xi, 98–99, 102, 104–105
World Café process, 123–124

Yates Mill Elementary School, xi, 88, 98–105

Zimmerman, D., 122

Leaders of Learning
Richard DuFour and Robert J. Marzano
Together, the authors focus on district leadership, principal leadership, and team leadership, and they address how individual teachers can be most effective in leading students—by learning with colleagues how to implement the most promising pedagogy in their classrooms.
BKF455

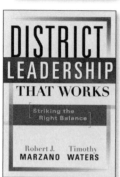

District Leadership That Works
Robert J. Marzano and Timothy Waters
Bridge the divide between administrative duties and daily classroom impact with a leadership mechanism called "defined autonomy." Learn strategies for creating district-defined goals while giving building-level staff the stylistic freedom to respond quickly and effectively to student failure.
BKF314

Leading a Learning Organization
Casey Reason
Improve the quality of organizational learning in your school. The author draws on educational, psychological, and neuroscientific research to show how leaders can change the prevailing emotional climate or tone of a school to promote deeper learning at all levels.
BKF283

The Future of Schooling
Bryan Goodwin, Laura Lefkowits, Carolyn Woempner, and Elizabeth Hubbell
The actions you take now will help your school or district succeed in the future. McREL experts show you how to use scenario planning to prepare for the future world of education, which will help you identify actions today that will maximize your chance for success tomorrow.
BKF433

More Than a SMART Goal
Anne E. Conzemius and Terry Morganti-Fisher
Successful school-improvement efforts not only set SMART goals, but also align them to the school-improvement process, curriculum, instruction, assessment practices, mandates, and professional development. Understand how to properly use the SMART goal process to effect change.
BKF482